APPLIED MARKETING

DONALD SCIGLIMPAGLIA
San Diego State University

JOHN WILEY & SONS
New York Chichester Brisbane Toronto Singapore

CONTENTS

PREFACE

The purpose of this book is to give students of marketing additional insight and experience in this field. The book contains many kinds of exercises and practical applications which should allow students to learn about marketing concepts and strategy.

To Students

This book is designed to help you learn about and expand your knowledge of marketing principles and practices. Most of the situations described in the exercises are based on real events and real firms, many of which you will recognize.

To Instructors

This book is designed to help you teach an introductory course in marketing. The exercises can be used in a variety of ways: 1) class homework assignments, 2) review exercises, 3) applications exercises and 4) basis of class discussion. Personally, I've found that daily exercises are a superior alternative to the "pop quiz", especially in large lecture classes. They can be collected daily or on a random basis to add an additional grading component. Answers to exercises and instructional comments are found in the instructor's manual for <u>Marketing</u>, although <u>Applied Marketing</u> can be used with any text. If you use a term paper as part of the course, note that a sample paper and a listing of information sources are included in this book.

Acknowledgements

I wish to thank Debbie Wartella, a former graduate assistant (now at Union Bank) for her help in locating materials for this book. Charles Goeldner of the University of Colorado and Kathleen Coleman of San Diego State University gave permission to use materials included in the Marketing Research Fact Finder. Suzanne Finnigan, a former student at the University of California, San Diego, wrote the term paper on Calvin Klein and designer jeans as a class project. Finally, I wish to thank Majorie Ulloa, who did an excellent job of preparing the manuscript.

Donald Sciglimpaglia

San Diego, California

MARKETING: WHAT IS IT?

Marketing is involved with activities which analyze and focus on consumers' wants and desires, resulting in the development of products and services based on this perspective. Also involved are communications and promotion activities as well as a wide range of distribution and pricing decisions. It might be said that effective marketing consists of a consumer oriented mix of business activities planned and implemented by a marketer (e.g., firm or organization) to facilitate the exchange or transfer of products, services or ideas so that both parties profit or benefit in some way. Thus, marketing is a function of both business and nonprofit organizations.

1. Describe the "marketing mix" for the following:

    a. Honda (automobiles)

    b. A public library

    c. Coca-Cola Company

    d. Planned Parenthood

2. What is the purpose or function of marketing for the following:

a. H & R Block tax preparation service.

b. General Motors Corporation

c. Your local college bookstore

d. McDonald's

MARKETING'S RELATIONSHIP WITH OTHER BUSINESS FUNCTIONS

Marketing is just one of the functions or activities that a firm performs.
Other functions include production, personnel and financial management.
Accounting and information systems are used to supply information to
assist these functional areas.

How would the following areas or functions of a firm be related to the
function of marketing? Be specific.

1.   Production management

2.   Financial management

3.   Accounting

4. Personnel management

5. Information systems/data processing

6. Research and development/product engineering

7. Quality control

COMPARING MARKETING ACTIVITIES

Antonio Vineyards is a small grape grower in California's Sonoma County wine country. The vineyard belongs to a grower cooperative which negotiates long term contracts with grape buyers, mainly large wineries. Under a growing contract, the vineyard can sell all of the grapes it can produce of specified varieties at a preset price. Since it takes years to produce mature grape vines, any change in the types of grapes it can produce is a long term process. Once the season's production is harvested, trucks belonging to the cooperative deliver the grapes to the contracted buyer.

E. & J. Gallo is one of the world's largest wine producers. Its brands of wine include Gallo, Boone's Farm, Spanada and Tyrolia. Gallo uses independent wholesale distributors to sell its products to retailers throughout the country. Multimedia consumer advertising is utilized to maintain awareness and brand appeal.

ABC Distributing is a wholesale distributor of wine and other distilled spirits in the Miami area. Its salesforce calls on retailers and restaurants in the area and, where appropriate, assists retail accounts in merchandising activities (e.g., displays) and special promotions. ABC maintains a large inventory of wines in its local warehouse and delivers orders using its fleet of trucks.

Courtesy Liquors is a local package store in the Miami area. Its owner determines what brands to carry and in what quantities. Most brands are priced at suggested list price, but sometimes the store will "experiment" with prices and special sales. The store does a little advertising in a neighborhood "shopper" newspaper and uses a listing in the yellow pages of the telephone directory. When asked to recommend a wine for a certain occasion, the owner will suggest particular brands.

Describe the process or function of marketing at each of the above firms.

1.   Antonio Vineyards

2.   E. & J. Gallo

3.   ABC Distributing

4.   Courtesy Liquors

LEGAL ENVIRONMENT OF MARKETING

A major external factor affecting marketing is the legal environment. Legislation and regulation exist at various levels. Some laws and regulations exist at the Federal level, in the U.S. or in foreign countries where a firm is involved in marketing activities. Others exist at the state level or the local level (i.e., city or county).

Consider the marketing of alcoholic beverages, distilled spirits, beer and wine. As you may already be aware, a wide variety of laws, rules, regulations and "guidelines" affect this industry. Virtually all elements of marketing decision making are involved, including advertising, distribution, product planning and pricing.

Below are a series of prohibitions or regulations concerning the marketing of alcoholic beverages. Indicate whether each is likely to be at the Federal, state or local level (or any combination). Check the appropriate spaces.

	Federal	State	Local
1. Certain counties in this state are "dry" and no alcoholic beverages can be sold.	_____	_____	_____
2. Beer and wine may be sold in local stores, but in this state liquor is sold only in state operated outlets.	_____	_____	_____
3. Wholesale distributors cannot sell to retail accounts outside of the state.	_____	_____	_____
4. In this area, you must be 21 years old to drink.	_____	_____	_____
5. Hard liquor (e.g., scotch) is advertised in magazines but not on television	_____	_____	_____
6. In this area, no alcoholic beverages are sold for "take-out" on Sunday.	_____	_____	_____
7. In this area, all bars must be closed by 2:00 a.m.	_____	_____	_____
8. In this area, all retailers must charge the same prices for hard liquor.	_____	_____	_____

		Federal	State	Local
9.	A product labeled as an "ale" can have a higher alcoholic content than one labeled "beer."	_____	_____	_____
10.	In France, the only sparkling wine which can be labeled champagne must be produced in the region of Champagne.	_____	_____	_____
11.	In this area, no alcoholic beverages can be sold within 1,000 yards of a public school or a church.	_____	_____	_____
12.	In this area, beer or wine can be purchased with a meal only if the patron joins a separate "club" which supplies the beverages.	_____	_____	_____
13.	A can or bottle of "light" beer must display the number of calories and carbohydrates per serving.	_____	_____	_____

Name _____

CHANGING MARKET DEMOGRAPHICS

Refer to U.S.A. Statistics in Brief (Appendix):

1. Compare the age mix of the U.S. population between 1970 and 1981. Compute the following percentages and supply the other required information:

	1970	1981
Median Age	_____	_____
Percent 65 or over	_____ %	_____ %
Percent 45 or over	_____ %	_____ %
Percent 35 or over	_____ %	_____ %
Percent 25 or over	_____ %	_____ %
Percent 18 or over	_____ %	_____ %
Percent 17 or under	_____ %	_____ %

What conclusions can you draw?

2. Compare area population figures in the U.S. between 1970 and 1981. Compute the percentages of U.S. population in each area:

	1970	1981
Northeast	_____ %	_____ %
North Central	_____ %	_____ %
South	_____ %	_____ %
West	_____ %	_____ %

What conclusions can you draw?

3. Compare household size in the U.S. between 1970 and 1981 by computing or supplying the following information:

	1970	1981
Average household size	_____	_____
Average family size	_____	_____
Percent of one-person households	_____ %	_____ %

What conclusions can you draw?

ANALYZING MARKET CHANGES

Refer to U.S.A. Statistics in Brief (Appendix):

What are the marketing implications of the following market statistics?
Compare the trends from 1970 to that of the most recent date and attempt
to identify an associated implication, such as a market opportunity or
problem.

	Market Factor	Most Recent Statistic	Trend
1.	Percent of adults who've completed high school	_____	_____
	Implication:		
2.	National unemployment rate	_____	_____
	Implication:		
3.	Percent of married women in labor force	_____	_____
	Implication:		

	Market Factor	Most Recent Statistic	Trend
4.	Median family income (constant dollars)	_____	_____
	Implication:		
5.	New housing units started	_____	_____
	Implication:		
6.	Cable system subscribers	_____	_____
	Implication:		
7.	Percent of single person households	_____	_____
	Implication:		

COMPARING DIFFERENT MARKET AREAS

Refer to U.S.A. Statistics in Brief (Appendix).

Compare the various statistical data for states and answer the following questions:

1.   Which state had the highest unemployment rate in 1981? Why?

2.   Which state had the highest per capita income in 1981? Why?

3.   Which state had the following characteristic:

      a. lowest per capita income   _____

      b. lowest unemployment rate   _____

      c. greatest population   _____

      d. least population   _____

      e. highest percent Spanish origin (Hispanic)   _____

      f. highest percent living in metropolitan area _____

      g. highest percent owner occupied dwellings   _____

      h. lowest percent owner occupied dwellings   _____

      i. highest population density   _____

      j. lowest population density   _____

THE DISCRETIONARY EFFECT OF RISING INCOME

As consumers' income rises, the proportion of income spent on various items or services may rise disproportionately. Income elasticity is an economist's term which measures the percent change in personal consumption expenditure for each one percent rise in real disposable personal income. Below are some recent income elasticity ratios:

Item	Income Elasticity
Total expenditures	0.97
Food at home	0.62
Restaurant meals	0.51
Alcoholic beverages	0.77
Shelter (housing)	1.16
Furniture	0.78
Radio, T.V., home electronics	2.21
Automobile purchases	1.33
Sporting goods, toys	1.71
Foreign travel	1.61
Higher education	1.55

1. Explain why food at home, restaurant meals and alcoholic beverages all have income elasticity figures below 1.0. Why do you think that restaurant meals is lowest of the three?

2. Explain why sporting goods, toys, foreign travel, higher education and home electronics have ratios much higher than 1.0. Why do you think that home electronics is the highest of this group?

3. Which product categories above would be most affected by a decline in real income in the U.S. Why?

Exercise 3.1   Name _____

IDENTIFYING MARKET OPPORTUNITIES

The first step in the development of a marketing strategy is the identification and evaluation of market opportunities. For example, the average size of the U.S. family has declined over time as parents have opted for less children. Is this a market opportunity?

Interestingly. toy manufacturers have noticed that while the average number of children per family has dropped, the average per child expenditure on toys has increased dramatically. This has created a great opportunity for producers who have responded with expanded product lines and the addition of "top of the line" toys.

1. Evaluate and identify the market opportunities below:

    a. A "packager" of travel tours and cruises notes that the average age of the population is increasing. In particular 26.3% of the U.S. population was 65 or older in 1981, compared to 10.0% in 1970.

    b. A national manufacturer of sporting goods notes the increase in interest in jogging and physical fitness.

2. The fastest growing ethnic category in the U.S. is the Hispanic or Spanish-speaking origin segment. Identify three separate market opportunities which would be related to this trend.

    a.

    b.

    c.

Exercise 3.2

Name _____

MARKETING STRATEGY AND TACTICS

Explain the following marketing strategies or tactics:

1. Johnson & Johnson has promoted some products designed for infants (e.g., baby powder and baby shampoo) to adults.

2. IBM has developed a less sophisticated version of its IBM personal computer, called the IBM PC Junior, for the home computer market, to compete with Commodore, Atari and Texas Instruments. The product plays games and is capable of running education and home-management software, but can handle only a limited version of the business software available for the IBM PC.

3. Anheuser-Busch has developed three separate brands of light beer: Natural Light, Budweiser Light and Michelob Light. Although Busch is the world's largest seller of beer, the light beer category is dominated by Miller's Lite brand. The light category now accounts for roughly 20% of the beer market and is growing at a steady rate.

4. Nike, a leading producer of athletic shoes, has recently launched a line of athletic clothing carrying the company brand and "swoosh" symbol. Although it hopes to sell the clothing items through its existing distribution outlets such as sporting goods dealers, it hopes to start making inroads with other retailers, such as clothing stores.

5. General Motors recently introduced the Cadillac Cimarron, the first subcompact car sold under the Cadillac name. The Cimarron is a luxury version of a basic subcompact sold in all other GM lines. For example, the basic price of the Cadillac version is a few thousand dollars more than the Chevrolet version, although the production costs differ by less than $500.

Exercise 4.1

Name _____

MARKET ANALYSIS: PICK A STATE

Very few products or services are purchased with uniform demand throughout the U.S. Per capita sales of many products vary greatly from region to region, due to such factors as geographical conditions, socio-economic variables, lifestyle and cultural differences. For example, consider the state of California. With about 10.6% of the population of the U.S., it is our most populous state. But it is a very good market for some products (i.e., per capita sales are greater than the U.S. as a whole) and a relatively poor market for others.

1. Consider the following products and services and estimate whether per capita sales in California are above or below the national average. Provide an explanation for your estimate related to market factors which influence demand.

		Above	Below	
a.	Wine	( )	( )	Your reason:
b.	Suntan lotion	( )	( )	Your reason:
c.	BMW cars	( )	( )	Your reason:

		Above	Below	
d.	Retail sales of gold coins and gold jewelry	( )	( )	Your reason:
e.	Vegetable shortening	( )	( )	Your reason:
f.	Legal services	( )	( )	Your reason:

THE MARKET GRID APPROACH

A useful method of visualizing market segments is the use of the market grid approach. This technique, attributed to Prof. E. Jerome McCarthy of Michigan State University, allows the marketing analyst to create a "picture" of the market which can help isolate useful segments of a larger market. Often, two segmentation variables are considered concurrently to form a grid or matrix of potential segments.

1. Consider the following market grid for women's clothing, in which age of the consumer and price category are both used to classify the market into segments (lettered A-I).

AGE CATEGORY OF CONSUMER

		Pre-teen	Teenager	Adult
PRICE	Budget	A	D	G
OF	Moderate	B	E	H
MERCHANDISE	High	C	F	I

What would be the most appropriate market segment(s) for each of the following? Circle the appropriate letters(s).

A. The budget basement shop of a major department store

    A D G
    B E H
    C F I

B. The women's wear department of Sears

    A D G
    B E H
    C F I

C. A specialty store which plans to carry "designer' clothing for younger girls

    A D G
    B E H
    C F I

D. A typical department store

    A D G
    B D H
    C F I

2. Now, consider the following market grid for microcomputers, classified by price range and expected use.

WHERE OR HOW USED

		In Schools	At Home	At Work
	Under $200	A	D	G
PRICE	$200 - $2000	B	E	H
	Over $2000	C	F	I

Answer the following questions by circling the appropriate letter(s) corresponding to market segments.

a. The Apple II and IIe are priced in the $200-$2000 range. What segment or segments should Apple consider for this product line?

A D G
B E H
C F I

B. Apple's "Lisa" introduced in 1983 for about $10,000 was designed with "integrated software", allowing the user to shift information from program to program and with an "electronic mouse" to minimize the need for inputing commands to the computer. The system contained programs for word processing, file management, project management and graphics.

A D G
B E H
C F I

C. Coleco's "Adam" computer system, introduced late in 1983 for about $600, has the capability to run entertainment programs and was delivered complete with word processing software and a printer.

A D G
B E H
C F I

Name_____

MARKET SEGMENTATION

In determining whether or not a market segment would make a viable target for a good or service it should possess several characteristics. Generally, to determine if a segment is meaningful it should:

1. have distinguishing characteristics which set it apart from other groups of consumers,

2. have significant market potential size relative to marketing objectives and potential profitability,

3. be accessible through specific promotion or distribution channels,

4. have a high likelihood of reacting favorably to a specially tailored marketing program or effort.

Below is a series of potential market segments and a product or service "targeted" for each. Consider each of the above criteria for all market segments and check below if you feel that the segment meets each criterion. Indicate any major problem(s) that you forsee for each proposed segment/product.

Market/Product	1	2	3	4
1. <u>Attenzione</u>, a proposed magazine for Italian Americans. Potential problem(s):	___	___	___	___
2. A line of kitchen tools designed for left-handers. Potential problem(s):	___	___	___	___

Market/Product	1	2	3	4

3. A new alcohol rehabilitation
   program for problem drinkers.   ____ ____ ____ ____
       Potential problem(s):

4. A nation-wide pay television
   program guide for cable subscribers.   ____ ____ ____ ____
       Potential problem(s):

5. A moderately priced resort designed
   solely for retirees and senior
   citizens.   ____ ____ ____ ____
       Potential problem(s):

6. An inventory control software
   package for retail shoe stores
   which runs on most microcomputers   ____ ____ ____ ____
       Potential problem(s)

7. A new fragrance designed
   exclusively for teenage girls.   ____ ____ ____ ____
       Potential problem(s)

                      Name _____

CONSUMER OF INDUSTRIAL GOODS

Identify whether each of the following is a consumer of industrial good or service.

		Consumer Good or Service	Organizational/ Industrial Good or Service
1.	Salt sold in bulk to a food products manufacturer.	_____	_____
2.	Salt sold in individual containers in a grocery store.	_____	_____
3.	Salt sold in single use packages to fast food restaurants.	_____	_____
4.	Salt sold in individual containers to a hospital.	_____	_____
5.	Salt sold to a food products wholesaler for resale.	_____	_____
6.	A passbook savings account at a local Savings & Loan.	_____	_____
7.	A loan to start a new business.	_____	_____
8.	A loan to finance a home remodeling job.	_____	_____
9.	Income tax preparation for an individual.	_____	_____
10.	Income tax preparation for a partnership.	_____	_____
11.	Paper clips purchased by a student at the college bookstore.	_____	_____
12.	Paper clips purchased by the college administration.	_____	_____
13.	Paper clips purchased by the bookstore for internal use.	_____	_____

MARKET SEGMENTATION STRATEGY

Four major segmentation strategies are undifferentiated marketing, concentrated marketing, differentiated marketing and custom marketing. Identify the proper market segmentation strategy in the situations below.

        A = Undifferentiated marketing
        B = Concentrated marketing
        C = Differentiated marketing
        D = Custom marketing

	A	B	C	D
1. A record company produces records for a variety of musical tastes (e.g., jazz, classical, country and western).	___	___	___	___
2. Another record company records and distributes only classical music.	___	___	___	___
3. The Ford Motor Co. produces the Ford Escort, which is sold worldwide as its basic subcompact automobile.	___	___	___	___
4. Ford produces multiple versions of the same automobile for different market segments (e.g., the Mercury Lynx and the Ford Escort).	___	___	___	___
5. BMW sells automobiles in the U.S. only in "luxury foreign compact" category.	___	___	___	___
6. A defense systems contractor develops weapons systems solely for the U.S. Department of Defense.	___	___	___	___

	A	B	C	D

7. A food services supplier specializes in providing airline meals to major air carriers.

8. Ford's Model T was designed as the universal automobile and was only available in black.

9. A public accounting firm specializes in providing services to the hotel/motel industry.

10. A computer software firm offers to develop specialty applications programs for any type of business.

WHAT IS A MARKET?

We might define a market as a group of individuals or organizations who may want to buy certain goods or services and who meet the following criteria:

    1.   They must have purchasing power
    2.   They must be willing to buy
    3.   They must have purchasing authority.

1.   Why is the advertising for some ready-to-eat cereals directed to children? Isn't this opposed to our definition of market criteria? (Explain.)

2.   A major advertising campaign for an alcohol treatment program is directed to the families of alcoholics. Is the market for this program the alcoholic, the family or both? Explain in light of the definition and market criteria above.

3.   A new word processing system for IBM is advertised heavily on national television, with the major thrust directed at secretaries. The campaign shows how the new system can make the secretary's job easier and more problem free. Does the secretary have "purchsing authority"? Evaluate this strategy in light of our definition of a market.

TYPES OF MARKETING RESEARCH

Marketing research is used to explore problem areas (exploratory research), to describe situations (descriptive research) and to find causes of particular situations (causal research).

Identify the type of research used in each of the following situations.

        1 = exploratory research
        2 = descriptive research
        3 = causal research.

1. Levi Strauss & Co. traces the sales of jeans
    at various retail outlets   _____

2. Levi Strauss conducts focus group discussions
    to investigate potential new product items   _____

3. Levi Strauss increases advertising expenditure
    in the St. Louis market to see if sales are
    significantly affected   _____

4. In order to determine the composition of the
    men's clothing market, Levi Strauss conducts
    a survey of 2,000 male consumers   _____

5. Fisher-Price Toys pretests new toy prototypes
    by observing children's reaction to them in a
    "preschool" run by the company   _____

6. McDonald's tracks attitudes toward fast food
    restaurants in a national survey of consumers
    conducted quarterly   _____

7. Safeway Stores reduces the price level on some
    private label products to determine price
    sensitivity compared to national brands   _____

8. An industrial manufacturer surveys purchasing
    agents to determine future buying intentions   _____

9. McDonald's conducts an internal research study
    to determine product sales by time of day   _____

10. McDonald's store employees are informally surveyed
    to attempt to discover potential reasons for
    poor performance of a new product, McFeast   _____

COMPARING SURVEY METHODS

The three major marketing research survey methods are mail, telephone and personal interviews.

1.   Which method has the following characteristic?

        1 = mail
        2 = telephone
        3 = personal

     a.   Most expensive per respondent   _____

     b.   Most likely to have potential influence
          by interviewers   _____

     c.   Allows most versatile questions   _____

     d.   Fastest data collection   _____

     e.   Allows longest questionnaire (most data)   _____

     f.   Gets best respondent cooperation   _____

     g.   Requires most standardized questionnaire   _____

     h.   Slowest speed of data collection per
          respondent   _____

     i.   Lowest cost per respondent   _____

2.   What survey method would you recommend for a study to be conducted for a manufacturer of contraceptive products. The survey is to be conducted with high school girls throughout the U.S. and will ask sensitive questions regarding sexual behavior. Explain.

3. What survey method would you recommend for a fast food chain which desires to determine recall and reaction to a new commercial which will air on network television? Explain.

MARKETING RESEARCH: EXPERIMENTATION

Design a marketing <u>experiment</u> to research each of the following situations. Explain the approach you suggest using the factor(s) that are controlled in the experiment and any major factors that are uncontrolled. Below is an example:

<u>Effect on unit pricing on sales</u>. A supermarket chain is interested in determining what effect would result by displaying unit price information (e.g., cost per ounce) along with the price of each item sold.

<u>Approach</u>: Select two matched samples of supermarket stores. In one sample continue to use only item pricing, while in the other also use unit pricing. If unit pricing has an effect, the brands or sizes purchased in a product category will probably be more "economical" in the stores employing unit price information. Therefore, sales of specific product categories by brand and size could be compared.

<u>Controlled and uncontrolled factors</u>: Select the stores such that the two samples are matched as much as possible. Each sample pair of stores should have similar sales histories, should be in similar types of neighborhoods and have similar types of area competitors. Keep prices and advertising the same for all the stores over the trial period.

A major uncontrollable factor would be the stores' competition. Would there be any major changes in pricing or advertising?

1.   Coors Brewing Company: Choosing the Right Advertising Campaign.

Coors Brewing Company recently decided to introduce a superpremium beer to compete with Budweiser's Michelob brand. The company's advertising agency suggested two alternative themes:

   Theme A: "One of the Best" - comparing the new brand to the best of any category mentioned.

   Theme B: "10" - comparing the new brand to beautiful women, rated on a ten-point scale.

Which advertising theme should be selected?

Approach:

Controlled and uncontrolled factors:

2. Banzai Beer: Testing a New Light Beer.

    The importers of Banzai Beer, a Japanese import, are considering the
    introduction of a new imported light beer. How would import and
    light beer drinkers react to its taste? The major competitors would
    be Heineken (import), Micheloeb (superpremium), Budweiser (premium)
    and Miller's Lite (light).

    Approach:

    Controlled and uncontrolled factors:

3. Safeway Foods: Determing the Effect of Shelf Placement.

    Management of Safeway Stores, a major supermarket chain, wants to
    determine how much shelf space to devote to certain private brands
    versus national brands. For example, should Safeway devote 10%, 15%
    or 20% of total detergent shelf space to its own brands?

    Approach:

    Controlled and uncontrolled factors:

COMPONENTS OF A MARKETING INFORMATION SYSTEM

A marketing information system (M.I.S.) contains three primary subsystems:
marketing research, internal records and marketing intelligence.

1. Provide an example of the use of each of three M.I.S. components for
    the following:

    a. <u>McDonald's Corporation</u>

        marketing research

        internal records

        marketing intelligence

    b. <u>Hertz Rental Car</u>

        marketing research

        internal records

        marketing intelligence

    c. <u>Miller Brewing Company</u>

        marketing research

        internal records

        marketing intelligence

2. What would be the components of a marketing information system for your college bookstore? Be specific.

Exercise 6.2

Name

SALES FORECASTING METHODS

A wide variety of sales forecasting methods are in use. These include: executive opinion, sale force composites, customer surveys, statistical trend projections and market factor analysis.

For each of the following, suggest a forecasting technique which you feel would be most appropriate. Explain your answer.

1. Panasonic is planning on introducing a novel product, a minature (1½" screen) color portable television. The new product would have a suggested retail price of $460.00

2. IBM needs to estimate the sales for a new software product to be sold to owners of the IBM PC. The product would be sold through computer dealers handling PC products.

3. GM wishes to project the size of the U.S. automobile market in 1990.

4. The producer of Dannon yogurt needs to forecast demand by retailers for the coming month in the Portland, Oregon market area.

Exercise 7.1

CULTURE

The term culture refers to the sum of values, expectations and norms of behavior of a society. With respect to consumer behavior, culture determines the social "acceptability" of products and activities.

In the U.S., how does culture affect the marketing of the following:

1.   Whole turkey and turkey products

2.   Horsemeat

3.   Firearms

4.   Shoulder bags ("man bags") for men

5.   Diamond jewelry

REFERENCE GROUPS

Groups which consumers use as points of comparison are known as reference groups. These include membership groups, those to which consumers are a part, and aspirational groups, those to which they aspire to belong.

What types of reference groups (both membership and aspirational) affect consumer behavior in the following situations? Be specific.

1. Clothing worn by high school sophomores.

2. Clothing worn by business school senior at an employment interview with IBM.

3. Choice of brand of tennis racquet purchased by intermediate skill tennis player.

4. Selection of a student's college major.

5. Type and brand of wine to order at a "posh" restaurant.

Exercise 7.3   Name _____

FAMILY DECISION MAKING

The term "family decision making" refers to how a family goes about making consumer behavior decisions, from what brand of toothpaste to buy to whether or not to buy a vacation time-share condominium. Certain decisions might typically be dominated by the husband, others by the wife and still others are made by husband and wife jointly (syncratic decisions).

1. For the following household decisions, consumer research suggests whether the husband or wife would be most involved or whether both are equally involved. Estimate the percentage of households in the U.S. in which the decision is dominated by the wife, dominated by the husband or is made jointly. For each situation your estimates should total 100 points.

Decision	Dominated by Wife	Dominated by Husband	Joint Decision
a. Choosing the color of a new refrigerator	_____ %	_____ %	_____ %
b. Selecting the brand of TV to buy	_____ %	_____ %	_____ %
c. Shopping at different automobile dealers	_____ %	_____ %	_____ %
d. Suggesting that a new TV be bought	_____ %	_____ %	_____ %
e. Deciding how much to spend for a new car	_____ %	_____ %	_____ %
f. Determining what brand of stereo to buy	_____ %	_____ %	_____ %

2. Assuming that your estimates above are correct, how might the results influence marketing decisions?

ATTITUDES

Consumer attitudes can be thought of as "predispositions to respond" in either a positive or negative way. An attitude can have three separate parts:

1.   Affective component (feelings)
2.   Cognitive component (knowledge or beliefs)
3.   Behavioral component (intended or actual behavior).

What attitudinal component is expressed by each of the following statements:

		Affective	Cognitive	Behavioral
1.	"Richard Nixon was a great foreign statesman."	____	____	____
2.	"I like Richard Nixon."	____	____	____
3.	"I would never buy a Fiat automobile."	____	____	____
4.	"Japanese cars are more reliable than American cars."	____	____	____
5.	"I prefer Honda automobiles overall."	____	____	____
6.	"Hondas have excellent resale value."	____	____	____
7.	"Next time, I think I'll look at Hondas when I shop for a car."	____	____	____
8.	"Potatoes are fattening."	____	____	____
9.	"I try to avoid eating fried foods."	____	____	____
10.	"Imported beers have higher alcoholic content than domentic beers."	____	____	____

PURCHASE DECISION MAKING

The decision making process of consumer behavior is often broken into five stages:

1.   Problem recognition
2.   Search for alternative solutions and information (risk minimization)
3.   Evaluation of alternatives (or choice criteria)
4.   Purchase decision
5.   Post purchase evaluation(cognitive dissonance)

Think of an important purchase decision which you have made (buying a car or stereo, deciding where to stay on a skiing vacation, etc.). Explain how you functioned at each of these steps in the decision. As much as possible, try to relate your answer to terms and concepts in the text's discussion.

Your decision: _____

1.   Problem recognition

2.   Search for alternatives

3.   Evaluation of alternatives

4.   Purchase decision

5.   Post purchase evaluation

FIND AN ADVERTISEMENT

Find an advertisement in a magazine or newspaper which is related to each of the following psychological aspects of consumer behavior. For example, an ad on the back cover of a magazine could be used to increase selective exposure. An ad for an insurance company portraying an anguished couple staring at the remains of their home after a fire utilizes a fear appeal.

Explain the application/illustration of the psychological concept you find in each ad. Staple the advertisement copies to this form.

	Concept	Advertisement For (Product/Service)	Explanation
1.	Safety needs		
2.	Self-actualization needs		
3.	Selective attention		
4.	Self concept		

5.   Problem recognition

6.   Evaluation of alternatives

7.   Attitude

8.   Brand image

9.   Perceived risk

PERCEPTION

One cognitive process of consumer behavior involves how we perceive products, brands and advertising. Associated with the perception process are selective exposure, selective attention and selective interpretation. In other words, a consumer is selectively exposed to various media or messages, pays attention to them selectively and interprets each selectively.

What aspects of perception are involved in each of the following situations? Explain.

1. The advertising director for Metro Bank is faced with the decision of what size ad to use for promoting a new service, Tele-Bank, in the local newspaper. She has narrowed the possible choices to a one-page ad or a two-page ad (at roughly twice the cost of one page).

2. Metro Bank's media coordinator is faced with a decision regarding where in the newspaper to place an ad promoting business loans and services. The advertising will stress the fact the Metro is the area's "most progressive business bank." Where should the ad be placed? Why?

3. Metro Bank's corporate management desires to develop the image in the community of being a progressive, modern institution. At a recent executive meeting someone suggested that the corporate logo (a shield on sky-blue background) is "too old-fashioned" and not consistent with this image. A senior vice-president dissented, saying that the existing symbol denotes "strength and security." What perceptual processes are involved here?

MOTIVATION

Needs or motives that consumers have are generally categorized into two major subsets: physiological and social or psychological. Abraham Maslow suggested a hierarchy of needs which exist at five levels:

    1. Physiological
    2. Safety
    3. Love or social needs
    4. Self-esteem
    5. Self-actualization

According to Maslow, consumer needs progress to higher levels only after those at lower levels are substantially met.

At what level in Maslow's need hierarchy are each of the following situations. Write in the appropriate number (1 though 5) from above.

1.   A gun purchased by a young woman for self protection.   _____

2.   A gun purchased by a husband to "protect the family."   _____

3.   A gun purchased by a collector as an addition to his
     collection.   _____

4.   A gun purchased by a wilderness recluse who intends
     to "live off the land."   _____

5.   A gun purchased by a city youth to impress his friends.   _____

6.   Life insurance purchased by a family man.   _____

7.   Smoke detectors.   _____

8.   Designer clothing.   _____

9.   Expensive French wines   _____

10. Clothing for pets   _____

INDUSTRIAL PRODUCTS

Match the following products and services with these categories of industrial goods.

    A = Raw materials
    B = Component parts
    C = Process materials
    D = Installations
    E = Accessory equipment
    F = Operating supplies
    G = Services

1. Paper clips purchased for office use.   _____

2. Salt purchased for the employee cafeteria.   _____

3. Salt purchased as an ingredient in
    processed foods.   _____

4. Computer disc drives purchased to be
    included as part of a microcomputer
    system.   _____

5. A forklift purchased for use in the
    warehouse.   _____

6. Advertising space purchased in a trade
    journal.   _____

7. Legal assistance obtained to review
    a contract.   _____

8. Typewriters purchased for the office.   _____

9. A $10,000 computer system purchased to
    run inventory control and data processing
    applications.   _____

10. Airline travel for company employees.   _____

Exercise 9.2

Name _____

PRODUCT LINES AND PRODUCT MIX

In this example we wil focus on the product mix of a major consumer goods marketer, Proctor and Gamble (P&G). Conduct an analysis of the follwing product lines of P&G. You will have to make one or more trips to local grocery stores for observation. First, determine P&G's brands in each product category (i.e., its product line). Next, try to determine how each separate brand is positioned (e.g., different market segments or product attributes).

1.   Product Line: <u>Laundry Detergents</u>

2.   Product Line: <u>Hand or Bath Soap</u>

BRAND NAME OR GENERIC NAME?

Some brand names become so popular or so commonly used to describe a product category that the marketer loses the exclusive rights to the trademark. Such a brand is called a generic name. Which of the following do you think are brand names versus generic names?

        B = Brand Name
        G = Generic product name

1.   Xerox   _____

2.   Shreaded wheat   _____

e.   Escalator   _____

4.   Thermos (bottle)   _____

5.   Real-lemon (lemon juice)   _____

6.   Aspirin   _____

7.   Kleenex   _____

8.   Frisbee   _____

9.   Jello   _____

10. Sanka   _____

11. Tylenol   _____

12. Noxema (face cream)   _____

13. Vaseline   _____

14. Crescent (wrench)   _____

15. Plexiglass   _____

16. Windex   _____

17. Velcro (fabric fastener)   _____

18. Band-aid   _____

19. Cellophane (tape)   _____

20. Barbie (doll)   _____

BRANDING

Characteristics of a good brand name include the following:

1.   It should be easy to remember.
2.   It should be easy to pronounce.
3.   It should have a positive connotation.
4.   It might be associated with product image.
5.   It might communicate product attributes or benefits.

Evaluate the following brand names:

1. Mr. Clean (cleaner)

2. Janitor-in-a-Drum (cleaner)

3. Spic 'N Span (cleaner)

4. Babe (fragrance)

5. Herbal Essence (shampoo)

6. Stir 'n Frost (cake mix)

7. Michelob (beer)

8. Crunchola (granola bars)

9. Soft 'n Dry (women's deodorant)

10. Nature Valley (granola bars)

11. Gee Your Hair Smells Terrific (shampoo)

12. Prime Time (shampoo for senior citizens)

13. Pringles (potato chips)

14. Roach Motel (cockroach trap)

15. Raid (insect spray)

16. Pierre Cardin (cologne)

17. Like (cola)

18. Lean Cuisine (frozen dinners)

19. Exxon (company name)

20. Xerox (company name)

PACKAGING

Packaging is an often overlooked topic by marketing students. To a product manager, however, a product's package can be used to help make it "stand out" at the retail level or can be used to help position the product with a specific target market. Importantly, even a basic product can be radically altered through the creative use of package design and shape.

This assignment is designed to get you to explore for yourself the marketing implications of product package decisions. Take the product categories suggested below (or another if assigned) and analyze the use of the package as part of the total product. To do this, you will have to make one or more trips to retail outlets for observation. Analyze the different "packages" used for various products or brands in the product category. Consider graphics, package design, size and special features which may have been designed as part of the packaging decisions.

1.   Product Category: <u>Wine</u>

2.   Product Category: <u>Women's deodorants</u>

3.   Product Category: <u>Breakfast cereal</u>

STAGES OF THE PRODUCT LIFE CYCLE

All products move through a life cycle which include the stages of introduction, growth, maturity and decline. Definition of each stage is related to factors such as market acceptance, sales growth rate, industry profits and the number and actions of competitors. Various stages will demonstrate differences in the number of product variations available, pricing, promotional activities and channels of distribution utilized. Your text has a complete discussion of the various stages of the product life cycle which you should study carefully before attempting this exercise.

Which stage do you think each of the following products is currently at? Explain your reasoning considering the factors discussed above and in the text. Be specific.

    I = introduction
    G = growth
    M = maturity
    D = decline

Product	PLC Stage	Reasons
1. Crisco shortening	_____	
2. Sony Watchman handheld TV	_____	
3. Imported bottled water	_____	

	Product	PLC Stage	Reasons
4.	Black and white television	_____	
5.	Morton's salt	_____	
6.	McDonald's restaurants	_____	
7.	IBM personal computer	_____	
8.	Manual typewriters	_____	
9.	"M*A*S*H" t-shirts	_____	
10.	Kerosene heaters	_____	

Exercise 10.2

Name _____

EXTENDING THE PRODUCT LIFE CYCLE

Many consumer products are in the mature stage of the product life cycle. An important challenge to the product manager is to try to find ways to sustain the sales of these products (i.e., extend the life cycle). Otherwise the product may slip into decline and may eventually be dropped. A number of marketing strategies can be employed. Below are a few:

1. Find new users for the product

2. Increase per capital consumption or usage among current users

3. Find new or novel uses for the product.

Assume that you are the product manager for each of the brands listed below and that you are designing your marketing strategy for the coming year. Sales for your product are leveling off and management is getting concerned. What do you recommend as possible ways to extend the life cycle of each. Be specific.

1. Quaker Rolled Oats

2. Lipton Iced Tea Mix

3. Gatorade Thirst Quencher

4.   Morton's Salt

5.   Brylcream Hair Cream

Exercise 10.3

Name_____

PRODUCT/MARKET STRATEGIES

Four basic ways of generating increased sales are described as 1) market penetration, 2) market development, 3) product development, and 4) diversification. Market penetration attempts to increase sales of present products to present customers or markets. Market development strives to increase or expand the markets for present products (e.g., international marketing) and product development expands the product assortment available to existing customers. Diversification seeks new products and new market opportunities.

Choose the best description of each of the following:

     A = market penetration
     B = market development
     C = product development
     D = diversification

1. Mattel decides to add a new wardrobe for the Barbie doll   _____

2. Mattel adds a new action figure (Smokin' Joe) to its line of dolls   _____

3. Mattel launches a new advertising campaign to attempt to expand its share of the action figure market   _____

4. Apple Computer Co. introduces the Lisa, a new product designed to allow Apple to be competitive in the executive computer market   _____

5. IBM reduces the price level on its IBM Personal Computer to increase demand   _____

6. Coca-Cola Co. introduces Diet Coke as its second sugar-free cola drink   _____

7. A computer software manufacturer translates a popular program into French, German and Italian for entry into the European market   _____

8. Lender's Bagels, a local manufactuer located in New Jersey, elects to try to ship its product line frozen to selected markets in the U.S.   _____

9. Burger King adds a salad bar in most outlets   _____

10. Wendy's offers a new bacon cheeseburger as an addition to the line of regular burgers   _____

PRODUCT LINE EXTENSION

A major method used to extend the product line and increase sales is by using what are called flanker products. A flanker product is an extension or variation of the existing product which is designed to expand the product's overall sales or to attract a slightly different market segment.

Some examples of flankers include Ocean Spray's expansion from cranberry juice into cranapple juice and now into non-cranberry juices. Ocean Spray is using its name recognition to capture an ever widening share of the juice market.

Assume that you're the product manager for the products listed below. Some currently have flankers and some do not. Suggest real or proposed suggestions for each product. Be specific.

1.   Kahlua Coffee Liqueur

2.   Nature Valley Granola Cereal

3.   Right Guard Deodorant

4.   Sara Lee Frozen Croissants

Exercise 10.5   **Name**_____

PRODUCT PORTFOLIO MATRIX

The concept of the product portfolio positions products on the dimensions
of relative market share versus market growth rate. Resulting product
portfolio categories are cash cows (high share, low growth), dogs (low
share, low growth), problem children (low share, high growth) and stars
(high share, high growth). The firm tries to balance its "portfolio" of
products by using funds from the cash cows to fund stars and problem
children and by moving away from products which are dogs.

Considering these dimensions and using the discussion in the text, give a
concrete example of each of these four product portfolio categories.
Carefully explain your reasoning for each.

1.   Cash cow

2.   Dog

3.   Problem child

4.   Star

Name _____

WHAT IS A NEW PRODUCT?

New product introductions exist on a continuum on newness of
1) discontinuous innovations, 2) dynamically continuous innovations and
3) continuous innovations. Discontinuous innovations are pioneering
products which are new to everyone. Dynamically continuous innovations
are new products which significantly alter buying or usage patterns.
Continuous innovations are relatively minor alterations to existing
products.

From the list below, determine the most appropriate innovation category
for each situation.

        1 = discontinuous innovation
        2 = dynamically continuous innovation
        3 = continuous innovation

1. The introduction of the first microwave oven
    by Litton   _____

2. The Sony Watchman, a handheld television receiver   _____

3. Coca Cola's introduction of Diet Coke   _____

4. Miller's introduction of Lite Beer   _____

5. Apple's introduction of the Apple II, the first
    widely marketed personal computer   _____

6. Hewlett-Packard's introduction of the first
    calculator watch (for $295)   _____

7. Casio's introduction of a solar powered calculator   _____

8. RCA's introduction of the video disc system   _____

9. Honda's introduction of a new automobile (the CRX)
    which replaces much body sheet metal with plastic
    to improve gas mileage   _____

10. The introduction of the cordless telephone
    (the Freedom Phone)   _____

OVERCOMING PROBLEMS WHICH INFLUENCE NEW PRODUCT DESIGN

A number of characteristics influence the adoption of new products. These include: 1) relative advantage over existing products, 2) the compatibility with existing consumption patterns, 3) triability, the ability to "test" the new product idea, 4) observability, the degree to which the adopter can see the "newness" of the product, and 5) complexity of the product.

Assume that you've been given the task of devising ways to influence the consumer adoption of several new products. Bearing in mind the five factors mentioned above, make suggestions for each of the following situations.

1.   A plastic surgeon in Los Angeles has devised a method of scalp hair transplantation which he feels will result in a more natural looking finished product for hair transplant patients. However, a potential patient must authorize the entire procedure at one time and some prospects have expressed reservations as to how the results will look. What do you suggest?

2.   A stereo manufacturer has developed a new type of stereo speaker system which it feels has superior acoustic properties. However, it is difficult for consumers to perceive the true difference in acoustic performance.

3. A manufactuer of agricultural chemicals has introduced a new product which, tests indicate, should increase corn production per acre. Corn farmers have expressed interest but have been slow to buy the product. The product is applied to the soil before the planting season and the results are not observed until harvest time. Some farmers expressed the concern of not being able to know whether or not the product works until it may be too late to use an alternative.

PRODUCT DEVELOPMENT PROCESS

Many firms develop new products using a multi-stage development process. These stages include 1) exploration, the search for new product ideas; 2) screening, a determination of the corporate "fit" of the proposed idea; 3) business analysis, an evaluation of potential profitability and returns; 4) development, the formulation or engineering of the actual physical product; and 5) commercialization, the market introduction of the product.

From the list below, select the appropriate stage of the product development process for each example:

        1 = exploration
        2 = screening
        3 = business analysis
        4 = development
        5 = commercialization.

1.   IBM's management attempts to determine if a new
      personal computer product idea is consistent
      with organizational goals and objectives.   _____

2.   3-M Company asks its sales force to be aware of
      novel applications of existing products which
      might suggest new product ideas.   _____

3.   Coca-Cola Co. conducts taste tests of Diet Coke
      to determine consumer acceptance prior to
      introduction.   _____

4.   Pocari, a Japanese thirt quencher product, is
      test marketed in several U.S. cities to evaluate
      marketability.   _____

5.   Apple Computer conducts a study to forecast the
      potential sales of a proposed consumer market
      version of its Lisa computer   _____

6.   A manufacturer of ready-to-eat cereals surveys
      consumers to find out what new cereal products
      they would like to see introduced.   _____

7.   A computer manufacturer asks its production
      engineering department if it has the capability
      to produce a proposed product.   _____

8. Quaker Foods Co. conducts a breakeven study to
    determine how many units of a proposed product
    would have to be sold to cover costs.   _____

9. Kodak develops trial versions of a new disc
    camera, which it gives to its employees for
    in-home use to evaluate product features.   _____

Exercise 12.1

Name _____

FUNCTIONS PERFORMED BY INTERMEDIARIES

Distribution intermediaries perform many functions for both producer and buyer. Consider the following example:

Coast Distributing Company is an independent wholesaler of beer products in a major west coast market area. Coast is also the exclusive distributor of Anheuser-Busch products, including Budweiser, Michelob, Natural Light, Bud Light and Michelob Light. In addition, Coast distributes four lines of wine and a number of brands of imported beer.

Match the situations listed below with the appropriate marketing functions performed by intermediaries:

```
 1 = break bulk
 2 = accumulate bulk
 3 = create asortment
 4 = reduce transactions
 5 = transportation
 6 = storage
 7 = exchange title
 8 = exchange information
 9 = provide required services
10 = extend credit
11 = risk taking
```

1. The importer of Kirin, a Japanese beer, needs to call on only one account, Coast, to service the market area. _____

2. Budweiser products are shipped in truckload lots from the brewery by Anheuser-Busch but delivered in any unit order the customer requests. _____

3. Coast delivers the product to retail accounts using its fleet of trucks. _____

4. Coast customer account managers assist retailers in setting up Budweiser displays. _____

5. Coast maintains a warehouse in the local area with the capacity to store the equivalent of one million single servings of beer. _____

6. Coast buys from a number of smaller importers to be able to extend a wide line of imported brands to retailers. _____

7. Retailers are invoiced by Coast on a "net 30 day" payment basis. _____

8. Coast sponsors local promotional events with retail
    accounts on behalf of Budweiser Light.   _____

9. Coast reports sales data by brand and by customer
    account to Anheuser-Busch.   _____

10. After being shipped to Coast, the product is owned
    by the wholesaler. If a problem were to occur later
    (e.g., loss of electrical power at the warehouse),
    it is Coast's responsibility to resolve.   _____

11. Coast "sells" the product of the producer, Anheuser-
    Busch, to the retailer. At the conclusion of a
    delivery call, the retailer owns the product in the
    beer cooler.   _____

ANALYSIS OF INTERMEDIARIES

Distribution intermediaries perform numerous marketing functions including breaking and accumulating bulk, creation of assortment, reduction in transactions, transportation, storage, exchange of title and information, extension of credit, provision of services and risk taking.

Select one wholesaler and one retailer in your area and describe the actual functions performed by each as indicated below:

Retailer (name and description)

Wholesaler (name and description)

FUNCTIONS

1.   Create Assortment

         Wholesaler:

         Retailer:

2.   Risk Taking

         Wholesaler:

         Retailer:

3. Provision of Services

    Wholesaler:

    Retailer:

4. Exchange Information

    Wholesaler:

    Retailer:

5. Transportation

    Wholesaler:

    Retailer:

6. Storage

    Wholesaler:

    Retailer:

7. Risk Taking

    Wholesaler:

    Retailer:

ALTERNATIVE CHANNELS OF DISTRIBUTION

Channel of distribution alternatives are numerous. The selection of the
appropriate channel depends on numerous factors, including characteristics
of the manufacturer (e.g., size, need for control), characteristics of the
product (e.g., unit value, perishability) and characteristics of the
market (e.g., size, concentration). Some of the major channel
alternatives include:

1. Manufacturer - Consumer (M-C)
2. Manufacturer - Industrial User (M-IU)
3. Manufacturer - Retailer (M-R-C)
4. Manufacturer - Wholesaler - Retailer (M-W-R-C)
5. Manufacturer - Wholesaler - Industrial User (M-W-IU)
6. Manufacturer - Agent - Wholesaler - Retailer (M-A-W-R-C)

Which do you think would be the most appropriate channel of distribution
for each of the following situations? Explain your reasoning thoroughly.

1. Software Prose, a small computer software producer is developing a
   new product, Financial Planner, which is designed to be used by
   professional personal financial planners. It would enable a
   financial planner to create balance sheets, cash flow summarizes and
   other reports for individual clients. The software has a suggested
   list price of $495.

2. Software Prose is also considering a less sophisticated version of
   its new program, called Home Planner, which could be used by
   consumers to help them manage their own financial affairs. The
   program is written to run on IBM and Apple type personal computer
   systems. It would list for under $100.

3. Funny Hats is a small company located in Honolulu. The company produces "novelty head wear" made of styrofoam. The basic product is a headband to which other pieces of colored styrofoam are attached in the shape or design of various animals or cartoon creatures. For example, it produces headgear in the shape of bumble-bees, fish, chickens and vultures. Its most popular product is a red lobster design complete with dangling "feelers." Its products are sold in a variety of retail outlets, such as novelty stores, costume shops, airport gift shops and college bookstores.

4. Maine-Frame-Systems is a firm in the Northeast which produces specialty computer software programs for financial institutions in the New England area. It specializes in programs designed to produce bank operations reports and customer account summaries.

VERTICAL MARKETING SYSTEMS

Vertical marketing systems can be described as corporate owned, administered by a channel member or contractual in nature. Contractual systems include retail cooperatives, wholesaler sponsored voluntary chains and franchise operations.

1. Which of the following types of vertical marketing terms best decribes the situations below?

> 1 = corporate
> 2 = administered
> 3 = retail cooperative
> 4 = wholesaler sponsored voluntary chain
> 5 = franchise

   a. Sixty-eight percent of all McDonald's outlets
       are owned and operated by franchisees   _____

   b. Thirty-two percent of all McDonald's outlets
       are owned and operated by McDonald's Corp.   _____

   c. IGA grocery stores are each independently owned
       and sell IGA private label products. These
       brands are supplied by a large food wholesaler
       which organizes the marketing activities of the
       IGA members   _____

   d. Century 21 real estate offices are each
       independently owned, but pay for the rights
       to belong to the real estate network   _____

   e. Sears is a major stockholder in many of its
       "independent" suppliers   _____

   f. Family Drug Stores is a group of independent
       pharmacies which combine their purchasing
       activities to generate volume discounts   _____

2. Conduct an interview with the owner or manager of a franchise operation. Determine how the franchise works as part of vertical marketing system. For example, what policies or activities are the responsibility of the franchiser compared to the franchisee?

EXTENT OF DISTRIBUTION

A decision regarding extent of distribution is the determination of density of retail outlets or distributors needed in order to gain adequate market coverage. A broad range of alternatives exist, with intensive distribution (maximum number of outlets to gain maximum product exposure) and exclusive distribution (exclusive market areas) at the extremes. Selective distribution, a middle strategy, involves limiting the number of outlets used to achieve more control than possible with intensive distribution.

What type of distribution coverage (intensive, selective or exclusive) would you recommend for each of the following situations? Explain your answer carefully.

1. Coca-Cola introduces a new product, Diet Coke. What should be the extent of distribution at the retail level? ... at the wholesale level?

2. Nakamichi is a brand of expensive, high quality stereo products. It is best known for a line of stereo cassette recorders which retail for about $500 to $2,500. What type of retail distribution coverage would you suggest? What questions should be asked to evaluate prospective dealers?

3. What type of distribution coverage should be recommended for selling Mercedes Benz automobiles in a large metropolitan area? How should Mercedes Benz determine the number of dealers required and their locations?

TYPES OF RETAILERS

Provide an example of each of the following retailing operations in your local area.

1. General merchandise retailer:

2. Single line retailer:

3. Specialty store:

4. Chain store:

5. Independent store:

6. Supermarket:

7. Department store:

8. Discount store:

9. Warehouse store:

10. Catalog retailer:

11. Non-store retailer:

ANALYZING RETAIL OPERATIONS

1. Select a moderate sized shopping center in your local area. List below up to twenty tenants of the center, the type of merchandise carried by each and a description of each as a retail operation (e.g., specialty store-independent).

Name and location of shopping center: _____

	Name of Store	Type of Merchandise	Retailing Description
1.			
2.			
3.			
4.			
5.			
6.			
7.			
8.			
9.			
10.			
11.			
12.			
13.			
14.			
15.			
16.			
17.			

	Name of Store	Type of Merchandise	Retailing Description
18.			
19.			
20.			

2. Which of the above stores offers the most customer services? (Describe)

3. Which of the above stores do you think sells at the highest gross margin? ... the lowest? (Hint: gross margin is selling price minus unit cost expressed as a percentage of selling price.)

4. Which of the above stores (question 1) do you think are complementary to one another? Does the business of one store increase the traffic at another?

TYPES OF WHOLESALERS

Full service wholesalers are those which perform a full range of services or functions as intermediaries. They are classified by degree of product specialization as general merchandise, general line or specialty wholesalers.

1.   Consult the yellow pages of the telephone directory and determine the name, location and telephone number of a wholesaler for each type listed below.

	Name	Address	Phone	Products
a. General merchandise wholesaler	_____	_____	_____	_____
b. General line wholesaler	_____	_____	_____	_____
c. Specialty wholesaler	_____	_____	_____	_____

2.   Conduct a short telephone interview with one of the above full-service wholesalers, determine what services or functions the wholesaler performs for the manufacturer.

2. Identify a limited-service wholesaler in your area (you may want to use the yellow pages again). Describe the wholesaler's operation and explain why you would classify it as a limited service or limited function intermediary.

3. Identify an agent intermediary in your local area and describe the services or functions performed.

PHYSICAL DISTRIBUTION

Select a product sold at a local store such as a supermarket. By asking questions and doing a little "marketing research" try to answer the following questions:

Product: _____   Store: _____

1. How does the store keep track of the amount of product available for sale?

2. Who does the reordering for the product? How often is it reordered and in what quantity?

3. In what unit size does the product arrive at the store (e.g., dozen or gross)? Where is it kept in storage at the store (if at all)?

4. How is the product delivered to the store (what mode of transportation)?

5. Is the product shipped from a warehouse or distribution center? If so, how is the product delivered there?

Name _____

TRANSPORTATION METHODS

Marketing managers and transportation or logistics specialists can choose
from a number of alternative modes of transportation. These include
1) motor carriers, 2) air freight, 3) railroads, 4) water transportation
and 5) pipelines.

These various modes of transportation can be compared on a number of
dimensions. Consider these:

    1. speed of delivery
    2. unit cost (weight/distance)
    3. dependability of service
    4. number of destination points served.

1. Rank each of the five modes of transportation on these service
    dimensions.

	Motor Carrier	Air Freight	Rail-road	Water Transpor-tation	Pipe-lines
1. speed of service (1=fastest)	____	____	____	____	____
2. unit cost (1=most expensive)	____	____	____	____	____
3. dependability (1=most dependable)	____	____	____	____	____
4. destination points (1=most destinations)	____	____	____	____	____

2. Why would a marketing manager ever use a more costly method of
    transportation. Explain.

3. What are some types of products that are likely to be shipped by:

a) air freight

b) pipeline

c) water transport

Exercise 14.3

Name _____

TOTAL COST CONCEPT

The systems approach to physical distribution assumes that marketing managers should treat physical distribution as a complex problem. As a system, managers strive to minimize the impact of individual physical distribution activities of total cost. This thinking is known as the total cost approach.

For example, in managing an inventory control system, two major cost components are the cost to order new stock (ordering cost) and the cost associated with carrying stock in inventory (carrying cost). One approach to determine how much to order at one time is called the economic order quantity (EOQ) model, which balances carrying costs against ordering cost.

Assume that annual demand (usage) for a product is 1200 units and that demand is relatively constant. Each item costs the firm $48.00. The cost to place an order (shipping, handling and order processing) averages $24.00 for each order placed. The cost to carry inventory is 12% per year. We need to know how many to order (Q).

Ordering costs per year equal the yearly demand divided by the average order (Q) times the ordering cost. Or, $(\frac{1200}{Q})(\$24)$.

Carrying costs per year equal the average amount in inventory $(\frac{Q}{2})$ times unit cost times percentage carrying costs. Or, $(\frac{Q}{2})(\$48)(.12)$. Total costs equals annual order costs plus annual carrying costs.

1. Compute the annual cost, carrying cost and total cost for the various order sizes (Q) below:

Order Size	Annual Ordering Cost	Annual Carrying Cost	Total Cost
400	$(\frac{1200}{400})(\$24)=\$72$	$(\frac{400}{2})(\$48)(.12)=\$1152$	$\$72+\$1152=\$1224$
200			
100			
50			
25			

What order size appears to minimize total costs? _____

2. A formula for computing the economic order quantity (Q above) is as follows:

$$Q = \sqrt{\frac{2 \text{ x annual demand x ordering cost per order}}{\text{cost per unit x carrying cost per year (\%)}}}$$

Substitute the figures given above in the formula and solve for Q.

3. What assumptions are being made which might limit the usefulness of the EOQ model?

PRICE VS. NON-PRICE COMPETITION

Price competition affects consumer demand by changes in price. Non-price competition allows the marketer to emphasize other marketing elements rather than using price decreases to attract customers.

Are the following examples of price or non-price competition?

    P = Price competition
    N = Non-price

1.   A marketer of professional seminars offers a two-day program on strategic planning for $500 per person, but reduces the price to $450 if two or more persons from an organization enroll together.   _____

2.   A university in the area offers a similar program at $500 per person but offers to let the participants sit in on future offerings of the strategic planning seminar at no charge.   _____

3.   A third supplier of professional seminars offers a two-day planning seminar for $350 per person.   _____

4.   A manufacturer of personal computers offers to extend the warranty period for new computer buyers from 90 days to one year.   _____

5.   Kaypro Corp. lowers the price of its Kaypro microcomputer from $1795 to $1595.   _____

6.   Kaypro adds additional software which is included in the $1595 list price.   _____

7.   Mazda provides below market financing (8.5% interest), available only for its line of lightweight trucks.   _____

8.   Chrysler offers a $500 per auto rebate to buyers of its Dodge Colt.   _____

9.   A manufacturer of office supplies offers a free jogger's watch for every organizational order of a gross of ballpoint pens.   _____

10.   A supermarket offers to give double the face value on grocery product coupons.   _____

PRICING OBJECTIVES

Match the following pricing objectives with the situations below:

        1 = Generate return on investment
        2 = Generate sales volume
        3 = Protect or improve market share
        4 = Stabilize prices
        5 = Avoid competition
        6 = Maximize long run profits
        7 = Match competition

1.   Sears reduces the price on selected hand tools 20%
     for a special two week sale.   _____

2.   Sears area managers are told to set overall prices
     such that each store will make a predetermined
     after-tax profit percentage.   _____

3.   A new entry in the home computer market prices
     below total costs in order to penetrate the
     market and gain market share.   _____

4.   Commodore reduces the price of its personal computer
     $50 to counter a $50 rebate offer from Texas
     Instruments for its product.   _____

5.   MCI prices a new business telecommunications service
     that it has pioneered very low, in order to prevent
     other future suppliers from undercutting the service
     rates.   _____

6.   ARCO does away with credit card transactions for
     gasoline at its ARCO stations and reduces the
     wholesale price to its dealers by seven cents
     per gallon.   _____

7.   ARCO dealers reduce retail gasoline prices an
     average of five cents per gallon below that
     of competitors.   _____

Exercise 16.1   **Name** _____

PRICE SETTING

1.   What would the breakeven quantity be for the following situation:

        Fixed cost $250,000.00
        Variable cost/unit $6.00
        Price/unit $25.00

2.   Assume that you are using the target return method of pricing. What would be the selling price for the following situation:

        Fixed cost $250,000.00
        Target return $50,000.00
        Variable cost/unit $6.00
        Expected demand   200,000 units

3.   Using the average cost method, what would be the selling price for the following situation:

        Production and marketing costs $300,000
        Margin for profit $50,000
        Expected demand   5,000 units

4.   Assume that you wanted to set a price which would yield a 10% pre-tax return of fixed costs. What would the price be for the following situation:

        Fixed cost $500,000.00
        Variable cost/unit $6.00
        Expected demand   200,000 units

5. For question Number 4 above, what would be the results if actual demand were only 163,000 units (at the price determined above)?

6. If the manufacturer's cost is $400, the selling costs are $50 per unit and you wished a 40% mark-up, what would be the price?

7. If a retailer buys a product for $40 and wants to set a price which would yield a 40% margin based on the selling price, what would be the price?

PRICING COMPARISONS

Choose a supermarket and a convenience store in your area and determine the selling price for each of the following products. By asking cooperative store managers or by using your best judgment, estimate the retailer's unit cost and percentage markup for each product.

Supermarket: _____
(name and location)

Convenience store: _____
(name and location)

	Product	Supermarket			Convenience Store		
		Unit Price	Unit Cost	Percentage Margin	Unit Price	Unit Cost	Percentage Margin
1.	Coca-Cola (12 oz., six pack cans)	____	____	____	____	____	____
2.	Crest toothpaste (6.4 oz.)	____	____	____	____	____	____
3.	Campbell's tomato soup (10½ oz.)	____	____	____	____	____	____
4.	Kellogg's cornflakes (10 oz.)	____	____	____	____	____	____
5.	Zest soap regular (5½ oz.)	____	____	____	____	____	____
6.	Visine eyedrops (1 oz.)	____	____	____	____	____	____
7.	Kodak 35mm print film (24 exposures)	____	____	____	____	____	____
8.	Pam cooking spray (8 oz.)	____	____	____	____	____	____
9.	Eggs, large (1 dozen)	____	____	____	____	____	____

PRICING TERMS

Explain the meaning of the following pricing terms:

a.   The price is $394.95 F.O.B. factory.

b.   The price is $394.95 with cash terms of (3/10 net 30).

c.   The price is $394.95 with chain discount terms of (30/10/5 net 30).

d.   The price is $394.95 per unit for purchases in lots of ten or less,
     $374.95 for purchases of eleven or more.

e.   The price is $394.95, $364.95 at the end of the season.

f. The price is $394.95 delivered east of the Rockies, $414.95 in the west

g. The price is $394.95 (net 45).

h. Promotional discounts

i. Trade discounts.

j. Cumulative quantity discounts.

PRICING STRATEGIES

1. Which of the following are typically sold with a one-price or a
    variable-price pricing policy? Why?

    a) Movie tickets

    b) Automobiles

    c) Stereo equipment (purchased at a department store)

    d) Airline tickets

    e) Income tax preparation service by a public accountant

2. Which of the following situations would typically imply either skimming or penetration pricing? Why?

a) Demand for the product is very price sensitive

b) A major competitor is able to enter the market in a short time

c) The product is unique

d) Demand is fairly inelastic

e) It is relatively easy for consumers to determine the value of the product

3. What are some other examples of total profit pricing in addition to razor blades and razors?

ELEMENTS OF PROMOTION

The four major elements of promotional are <u>personal selling</u>, <u>advertising</u>, <u>publicity</u> and <u>sales promotion</u>. Personal selling involves direct face-to-face selling efforts and telephone marketing activities. Advertising is paid communications designed to inform, persuade or remind consumers. Publicity is unpaid communications by which the marketer attempts to benefit. Sales promotion is a catch-all term which describes various activities other than personal selling, advertising or publicity. In many cases sales promotion involves temporary offers of material reward.

        1 = personal selling
        2 = advertising
        3 = publicity
        4 = sales promotion

1. Continental Airlines announces a short-term
    "come and get it" fare of $49 for any
    direct flight on its schedule.   _____

2. Continental Airlines calls a press conference
    to explain its reasons for declaring bankruptcy
    and seeking reorganization.   _____

3. Continental Airlines instructs its reservations
    operators on how to suggest flights from its
    schedule as opposed to its competitors.   _____

4. Continental Airlines invites a group of travel
    agents from around the country to fly free on a
    Continental flight to "experience our superior
    service."   _____

5. Continental Airlines takes out a series of
    newspaper ads to explain its new fare schedule.   _____

6. United Airlines uses a "frequent flyer" program
    which enables persons who fly a certain number
    of miles on United to win free travel privileges.   _____

7. Republic Airlines tries to increase demand on its
    Denver-Houston flights by upgrading the meals
    served on these flights only.   _____

8. Republic Airlines announces the upgraded meals on
    billboards in Denver and Houston.   _____

9. Republic Airlines invites the travel editors of
    local newspapers in Denver and Houston to fly
    between the two cities to sample the food service
    (steak and lobster) and to stay overnight at the
    airline's expense.   _____

10. Customer representatives are sent to call on travel agents in Houston and Denver to inform agents of the change in service.   _____

11. Travel agents are given coupons which can be redeemed for a free bottle of wine on Republic's Denver-Houston flights for selected customers of the travel agencies.   _____

12. United Airlines offers a free flight coupon which can be redeemed for future air travel to anyone flying on certain flights.   _____

13. American Airlines runs an in-flight "game" which allows customers who win to upgrade a future flight from coach to first class.   _____

USE OF PROMOTION

Consider a fast food franchise such as McDonald's. Based on your recent experience or observation, how does the franchise use each element of promotion: personal selling, advertising, publicity and sales promotion?

Name of fast food franchise: _____

1. Personal Selling

   How does the franchise use personal selling? Can you recall any specific examples of selling efforts at the store level? Discuss.

2. Advertising

   Think of some recent uses of advertising. What media were used? What were the themes? What was the purpose of each ad or commercial?

3. Publicity

   Can you think of any examples of the use of publicity (or, perhaps, public relations)?

4.   Sales Promotion

What are some recent examples of the use of sales promotion? What
was the purpose of each of these activities?

COMMUNICATIONS PROCESS

Communications as a process defines "who says what to whom?" The process model of communications involves the following elements or factors:

1. the source
2. encoding the message
3. the transmission channel
4. decoding the message
5. the receiver
6. feedback
7. noise.

In each of the following scenarios, identify the communications elements specified.

1. Big Bear Supermarkets wants to try to reposition itself as the local supermarket chain with highest quality for the money. It develops a television advertising campaign which uses a celebrity to explain that Big Bear is the area's "... place where smart shoppers shop." A television viewer sees the commercial and comments to herself that, "Big Bear must be where the snobbish people buy groceries." She returns to the story that she's reading in <u>True Confessions</u>.

    a) source _____

    b) encoding _____

    c) transmission _____

    d) decoding _____

    e) receiver _____

    f) noise _____

2. The maker of Chanel Number 5 perfume develops a television advertising campaign around the theme of "Share the fantasy ... of Chanel Number 5." It features a series of surrealistic scenes (including a swimming pool sequence in which the shadow of an overhead airplane becomes superimposed with the figure of a male swimmer) designed to simulate thoughts of fantasy with a sexual undertone. A young woman watches the commercial and later buys a bottle of the perfume. Her boyfriend watches the same commercial, turns to her and says, "What does it all mean?"

a) source _____

b) encoding _____

c) transmission _____

d) decoding _____

e) receiver _____

f) feedback _____

PURPOSES OF PROMOTION

Promotion has three major purposes:

    1.   to inform
    2.   to persuade
    3.   to act as a reminder.

For this assignment, find an advertisement from the newspaper or in a magazine which illustrates each type of promotional purpose.

Attach the advertisements to this form (staple) and explain each promotional message in the space below.

1.   Information Ad

2.   Persuasion Ad

3.   Reminder Ad

PUSH VS. PULL STRATEGY

A push strategy is a promotional strategy that aims at the channel of distribution (for example, offering special price incentives to retailers). A pull strategy aims at consumers, with the hope that consumer demand will "pull" the product through the channel.

1. What are three separate "push" strategies that could be used by a manufacturer of stereo equipment?

    Strategy 1

    Strategy 2

    Strategy 3

2. Cite three separate examples of "pull" strategies designed to direct consumers to a dealer or to develop consumer demand. Be specific.

Strategy 1

Strategy 2

Strategy 3

Exercise 19.1   Name _____

LOCATING AND QUALIFYING PROSPECTS

An important initial step in the creative selling process is the location
of potential sales prospects. Good "sales leads" may come from
directories, lists, suggestions from other customers, promotions or other
sources. In an attempt to determine if the prospect is a good candidate
for a sale, the sales person should determine that a need exists for the
product, that the person contacted is in a position to make or contribute
to the buying decision and that he/she has the required budget and is able
to authorize the expenditure.

Assume that you're a field sales representative for an office equipment
distributor which has just added to its product line a new product, the
Type Master system, which turns almost any electric typewriter into a word
processing system. The system works this way: A typist types on a
computer-type keyboard containing a single-line display of the work and a
computer chip which contains a word processing program. The text is
stored on a standard cassette tape recorder until ready for printout. An
attachment causes the text to be "typed" by the electric typewriter, after
the typewriter has been slightly modified by the addition of a computer
interface. The whole system (keyboard with display, recorder, cables and
interface) costs $1,395 installed including an extensive training manual.
This price is at the extreme low end of the range for true word
processors. Thus, any small firm or office can turn its existing
typewriters into a letter-quality word processing system for under $1,400.

1.   What are five separate sources which you could use to locate
     prospects in your local area for the Type Master? Be specific.
     Identify how you would use each source.

     a.

     b.

c.

d.

e.

2. Assuming that you've generated a list of "sales leads" above, who (what persons) would you want to call upon at each firm/office? Why?

3. A true prospect should meet a three-part test: 1) is there a need for the product? 2) does the prospect have authority to buy? and, 3) does the prospect have the ability to pay? What questions should you ask to meet this test? Be specific.

HANDLING OBJECTIONS

A major part of the creative selling process is the handling of objections or complaints by the intended customer. A key point is to consider the objection to be a marketing opportunity. In many instances the seller can answer the objection in a positive manner, thus turning the point around to the advantage of the selling.

Assume that you're a field sales representative for an office equipment distributor which has just added to its product line a new product, the Type Master system, which turns almost any electric typewriter into a word processing system. The system works this way: A typist types on a computer-type keyboard containing a single-line display of the work and a computer chip which contains a word processing program. The text is stored on a standard cassette tape recorder until ready for printout. An attachment causes the text to be "typed" by the electric typewriter, after the typewriter has been slightly modified by the addition of a computer interface. The whole system (keyboard with display, recorder, cables and interface) costs $1,395 installed including an extensive training manual. This price is at the extreme low end of the range for true word processors. Thus, any small firm or office can turn its existing typewriters into a letter-quality word processing system for under $1,400.

How would you suggest handling the following objections:

1.   "Word processing is only for big companies. Small companies like ours can't use it."

2.   "Word processing won't work here because we don't know anything about computers."

3. "It's too expensive".

4. "I've heard that word processing is complicated and hard to learn."

5. "We have a lot of turnover among our secretary-typists. We'd have to do a lot of retraining after we lose an experienced person."

Exercise 19.3

SALES COMPENSATION

A wide variety of compensation plans are used to compensate sales force members. The individual plans range over a continuum from straight salary to straight commission, with a variety of combination plans in between. These combination plans include commission with draw, quota-bonus and salary plus commission.

Which of the following plans would you recommend in each situation below: Explain your reasoning.

        1 = straight salary
        2 = straight commission
        3 = commission with draw
        4 = quota-bonus
        5 = salary plus commission

1. Selling used cars at a local auto dealer   _____

2. Identifying and qualifying prospects for office
    copier sales (to be closed by someone else)   _____

3. Calling upon qualified prospects and (hopefully)
    closing sales for office copiers   _____

4. Calling upon physicians to "detail" a pharmaceutical company's products   _____

5. Selling expensive men's clothing at a local clothing store   _____

6. Selling record albums at the music department of a local department store   _____

7. Selling vacuum cleaners door to door   _____

8. Selling new airplanes to commercial airlines   _____

ADVERTISING MEDIA

Advertising media include local newspaper, magazines, radio, television and outdoor.

What would be your advertising media recommendation for each of the following situations? Explain your answers.

1. To announce the addition of a new line of office copier machines by an office products distributor in Tulsa.

2. To introduce a new breakfast cereal to children.

3. To inform mothers of the superior nutritional benefits of a new children's cereal.

4. To inform local customers of the sale prices of merchandise at an appliance store.

TYPES OF ADVERTISING APPEALS

A wide variety of appeals may be used in advertising. Find an example of each of the following types of appeals in magazines or newspapers and explain the function of each in the space provided. Staple the advertisements to this form.

1.   Product usage/problem solution.

2.   Testimonial.

3.   Comparison.

4.   Life-style.

5.   Demonstration of product attribute.

6.   Storyline.

ADVERTISING OBJECTIVES

Advertising can be used to reach many possible objectives. Using magazines and newspapers, find examples of advertisements which you think have the following objectives. Staple the advertisements to this form and explain each in the space provided.

An advertisement designed to:

1.   Introduce a new product.

2.   Remind current customers of an existing product.

3.   Stimulate short term demand by motivating immediate action.

4.   Change or reinforce consumer attitude.

5.   Attract buyers of a competitive product.

6.   Inform current customers of new uses for a product.

7.   Expand   the   current   market   for   a   product   by   appealing   to nontraditional users or new market segments.

Exercise 21.1   Name _____

CHARACTERISTICS OF INDUSTRIAL MARKETS

Industrial market demand can be described as being derived, relatively inelastic and fluctuating compared to the consumer market. The industrial market can be characterized as being more concentrated, in terms of numbers of buyers and location. Industrial buyers are more likely to buy direct and have more expertise and sophistication in buying.

Consider the following aspects of industrial market demand.

1. Derived demand

    How does the construction and sale of new homes in the U.S. affect the demand for related industrial products and services? What kinds of products or services are affected? (Be specific.)

2. Inelastic demand

    Comment on the relative elasticity of demand for each of these components of new home construction.

    a. The city council raises building permit fees by 20%.

    b. A supplier of roofing materials raises prices by 20%.

3. Concentrated markets

Where do you think that the market would be geographically concentrated for sales of:

a. automobile tires for new autos

b. raw materials used for domestic steel production

c. disc drives used as component parts for microcomputers

BUYING CENTER AND INDUSTRIAL BUYING

Multiple influences are the norm in industrial buying situations. Those involved in the buying process (i.e., the "buying center") play various roles, including users, gatekeepers, influencers, deciders and buyers.

Consider the case of HiTech Products, a relatively small manufacturer of precision electronic equipment. The company employs roughly 300 persons, including engineers, salespeople, technicians, production persons, clerical staff and administrators. Who in the firm might be involved in the buying process or as members of the buying center in each situation below. Be as specific as possible.

1. The office staff at HiTech primarily uses IBM typewriters. Typists seem to be satisfied with the IBM products and the typewriters are serviced under an IBM service contract. A number of manufacturers are now producing competitive products, notably electronic typewriters, which offer superior features for the same price as a new IBM model. HiTech is now considering upgrading some office typewriters or buying some additional ones.

2. HiTech is now considering the purchase of a minicomputer system to be used for production management, inventory control, billings and administrative use.

3. Many HiTech products are packaged in metal casings. For example, a precision instrument used in hospitals and clinics to monitor body functions is enclosed in a metal case. Currently HiTech buys all of the cases from a single supplier. A competitive supplier is now offering to supply metal cases made with a less costly process at a significantly reduced price. The new process yields a finish which is somewhat inferior to that of the metal cases currently purchased. The new supplier has been known to miss shipment dates and to have had some problems with product quality control. By switching to the new supplier, HiTech could save about $60,000 a year.

CLASSES OF INDUSTRIAL GOODS

Industrial goods and services can be classified into various product categories. These include:

    1. raw materials
    2. installations
    3. fabricating materials or component parts
    4. process materials
    5. accessory equipment
    6. operating supplies
    7. services

Using the numbers above, identify the proper category or class of industrial goods in each situation below:

1. Acid used to "bathe" computer chips under production   _____

2. IBM office typewriters   _____

3. IBM main frame computer system   _____

4. IBM computer cards   _____

5. IBM extended warranty on office equipment   _____

6. "Rent-a-plant" office plants   _____

7. Landscaping design for new office complex   _____

8. Paper towels for the office complex   _____

9. Industrial solvents used in production process   _____

10. Lumber used to frame new office complex   _____

11. Batteries purchased for hand held video games   _____

12. Petroleum used to produce gasoline   _____

13. Screws used to assemble video game console   _____

Exercise 22.1   Name _____

RESEARCHING A FOREIGN MARKET

Once a company decides to embark on a policy of international marketing it
obviously must investigate the market potential of foreign markets.
Demographic considerations include population size, population growth
rate, family size and age distribution. Economic factors include
household income, economic growth rate, state of economic development,
inflation rate, imports and exports and competitive activity. Political
and legal considerations include type of government, degree of stability,
legal barriers to entry and political regulations on business. Cultural
factors include custom and language.

Conduct a short library research project on a foreign country, analyzing
it as a possible foreign market. Attach your report to this form for
completion of the assignment.

Some example foreign countries are listed below:

Ireland	El Salvador	South Africa
Italy	Colombia	Angola
West Germany	Peru	Zaire
Japan	Brazil	Libya
Belgium	Egypt	Israel
Hungary	Iraq	Australia
Poland	Kuwait	Indonesia

THE UNITED STATES AS A FOREIGN MARKET

For an export marketer in another country, such as Japan or Germany, the U.S. is a foreign market. Consider what it must be like to learn to adapt to our market environment in order to be successful.

1. Try to list ten different consumer products which are exported to the U.S. market. (Try to identify ten different brands and product categories.)

        <u>Brand</u>   <u>Product Category</u>

  1. _____

  2. _____

  3. _____

  4. _____

  5. _____

  6. _____

  7. _____

  8. _____

  9. _____

10. _____

2. How have these exporters adapted to the U.S. market?

From your list above consider any special adaptations which were probably necessary to market the product in the U.S. Which of these probably required a substantial change in the product itself or in other aspects of the marketing mix? Explain.

MAKING INTERNATIONAL MARKETING DECISIONS

What information whould you require before deciding whether or not to market the following products? What information would be required in order to develop a marketing plan for each situation?

1.   IBM is considering the marketing of the IBM PC in West Germany.

2.   Mattel Toy Co. is considering the export of its line of dolls and action figures (e.g., Barbie, Ken and G.I. Joe) to Great Britain.

3.   Procter & Gamble (P&G) is considering the introduction of Pampers, a line of disposable diapers, to South America. Because of the unit shipment costs involved, P&G would most likely produce the product somewhere in that region, rather than export from the U.S.

CONSUMER ATTITUDES CONCERNING ADVERTISING

Many consumers consider advertising to be synonymous with marketing.
Conduct an informal survey of four or five average consumers to
investigate the following questions:

1. What television commercials do they find the most offensive or
   annoying?

2. What commercials do they feel are deceptive or unfair to
   consumers?

3. Are there any product categories or services which are now
   promoted on television which they feel should be banned?

Discuss your findings below:

TERM PAPER PROJECT

A good way to develop a thorough understanding of the practice of marketing in the "real world" is by conducting research on a particular product or company and writing a paper dealing with the marketing programs involved. This exercise dictates integrating a wide variety of facts and details about competition, consumer demand, market segments and marketing strategy.

As a guide to finding information for your report, a guide to secondary information sources, the Marketing Research Factfinder, is included. It lists a number of good sources which you're likely to find in the library. In addition, a sample student term paper, on Calvin Klein designer jeans, is included as a guide.

Your paper should include information about the following:

1. The company and product.

2. The market, including market segments, market demand and factors influencing demand.

3. The industry, including an analysis of competition.

4. The marketing program.

    a. product strategy
    b. distribution
    c. pricing
    d. promotion

MARKETING RESEARCH FACTFINDER

by

DR. DONALD SCIGLIMPAGLIA

MARKETING RESEARCH FACT FINDER*

This list should serve not only as a guide to free and inexpensive sources of management information for research and planning purposes, but also as an "eye-opener" to the wealth of available data that is yours for the asking. Effective utilization can save hours of time and provide useful information that might otherwise be missed.

I. General Sources

Obviously, the first place to look is the library. However, you can save yourself a great deal of time if you know what you are looking for. The first place to head is an indexing service.

A. Indexing Services

1. F & S Index of Corporations and Industries. (Cleveland: Predicasts, Inc., weekly, with quarterly and annual cumulations.)
Indexes company, product and industry information from over 750 business publications. Section One, covering products and industries, is arranged by SIC number. Section Two, covering individual companies, is in alphabetical order by company name.

2. Business Periodicals Index. An accumulated subject index covering approximately 170 periodicals in the fields of accounting, advertising, public relations, automation, banking, communications, economics, finance and investments, insurance, labor, management, marketing, taxation, and specific businesses, industries and trades.

3. Readers' Guide to Periodical Literature. Indexes the contents of the nation's general magazines.

4. Public Affairs Information Service Bulletin. A selective list of the latest books, pamphlets, government publications, reports of public and private agencies, and periodicals relating to economic and social conditions, public administration and international relations.

5. Economic Abstracts. Semimonthly review of abstracts of books and reports on economics, finance, trade and industry, management and labor.

---

*Based in part on C.R. Goeldner and Laura Dirks, "Business Facts: Where to Find Them," MSU Business Topics (Summer 1976) and Kathleen Coleman, "Basic Sources on Marketing," unpublished manuscript, San Diego State University Library;, 1977. The author gratefully acknowledges the permission to use these materials.

6. Applied Science and Technology Index. A cumulative subject index to periodicals in the fields of aeronautics, automation, chemistry, construction, electricity and electrical communication, engineering, geology and metallurgy, industrial and mechanical arts, physics, transportation, and related subjects.

7. The Wall Street Journal. An index listing all articles that have appeared in the publication.

The New York Times Index, The Engineering Index, The Agricultural Index, Psychological Abstracts, Advertising Age Editorial Index and Sociological Abstracts are other illustrative examples of indexes.

B. Periodicals

Illustrative of business periodicals are

Business Week, Forces, Fortune, Dun's Reviews, Nations Business, Newsfront, Harvard Business Review, Industrial Marketing, Advertising Age, Sales Management, Marketing/ Communications, Journal of Marketing Research, Journal of Retailing, Journal of Marketing, Journal of Advertising Research, Media Scope, Distribution Age, Journal of Business, Journal of Finance, Modern Packaging and many others. In addition, there are hundreds of trade publications covering almost every field.

The sources of locating these are

1. Ulrich's International Periodicals Directory. (New York: R.R. Bowker Co.) Includes entries for over 40,000 in-print periodicals published throughout the world.

2. Ayer Directory of Publications. (Philadelphia: N.W. Ayer and Son, Inc. annual.) Comprehensive listing of approximately 21,700 newspapers and periodicals.

3. Business Publications Rates and Data. (Skokie, Illinois: Standard Rate and Data Service, Inc., monthly.) Also lists publications by trade or professional categories.

C. Trade Associations

Don't overlook trade sources. Many trade associations maintain research departments and collect basic data on sales, expenses, shipments, stock-turnover rates, bad-debt losses, collection ratios, returns and allowances, net operating profits, market share, consumer profiles and significant trends.

To locate trade associations, check

1. Judkins, Jay. Directory of National Associations of Businessmen. (Washington, D.C.: U.S. Department of Commerce.)

2. Encyclopedia of Associations. (Detroit: Gale Research Co.)

3. National Trade and Professional Associations of U.S. 1970. (Washington, D.C.: Columbia Books, Inc.)

4. Directory of Trade and Professional Associations of the United States and Trade Unions.

D. Business Directories

1. Moody's Manual of Investments. (New York: Moody's Investor Service, Inc.) Contains a brief history of each company and its operations, description of products and plants, names of officers and five years or income accounts.

2. Standard and Poor's Register of Corporations, Directors, and Executives. (New York, annual, with three supplements.)

   Lists 37,000 corporations. In three volumes: vol. 1, corporate listings indicating address, telephone numbers, officers, accountant, sales, number of employees, SIC number, products and subsidiaries; vol. 2, biographical register of executives; vol. 3, indexes.

3. Thomas' Register of American Manufacturers. (New York: Thomas Publishing Co., annual.) Directory classified manufacturers by product. Includes alphabetical list of trade name index. (In general gives information on companies incorporated for less than one million dollars.)

4. Reference Book of Dun and Bradstreet. (New York: Dun and Bradstreet, Inc., bimonthly.) This reference book gives names, lines of business, Standard Industrial Classification code numbers, and credit and financial ratings of over 3 million business establishments in the United States and Canada. These are manufacturers, wholesalers, retailers and other businesses that buy on credit. Each listing contains five or more elements of information. The Reference Book is revised every two months. Sectional editions are also available.

5. Middle Market Directory. (New York: Dun and Bradstreet, annual.)

   Lists corporations with a net worth of $500,000 to $999,000. Gives address, telephone number, sales, number of employees, names of officers or directors and line of business. In four sections; businesses alphabetically, businesses geographically, product classification and D-U-N-S number classification.

6. <u>Million Dollar Directory</u>. (New York: Dun and Bradstreet, annual.)

Lists firms with a net worth of $1,000,000 or more. Format and arrangement are like those of <u>Middle Market Directory</u>, except that <u>Million Dollar Directory</u> has an additional section listing top management personnel.

7. <u>Directory of Corporate Affiliations</u>. (Skokie, IL, National Register Publishing Co., annual.)

Lists approximately 3,400 parent companies with all divisions and subsidiaries. Index leads from name of division or subsidiary to parent corporation. Very useful when the name of a parent firm must be identified when only the name of the subsidiary is known.

E. Directories of Trade Names

Often the name of the firm is not known, only the product or trade name. In that case check

1. Crowley, Ellen T., ed. <u>Trade Names Directory</u>. (Detroit: Gale Research Co., 1976.)

A guide to brand, product and other trade names for consumer products. Gives company names and addresses for brand names.

2. <u>Television Sponsors Directory</u>. (Everglades, FL: Everglades Publishing Co., quarterly.)

Identifies the companies behind advertised products, and gives the addresses of parent companies.

Another useful source is the <u>Standard Directory of Advertisers</u> below.

F. Advertising Directories

1. <u>Standard Directory of Advertisers</u>. (Skokie, IL: National Register Publishing Co., annual, with monthly supplements.)

Lists more than 17,000 firms advertising nationally or regionally. Includes firm name, address, telephone, officers, trade names of products, advertising agencies and media used, and amount of annual billings. Indexed by firm name, geographical location, trade names and products.

2. <u>Standard Directory of Advertising Agencies</u>. (Skokie, IL: National Register Publishing Co., three times annually, plus supplements.)

Lists 4,000 U.S. and 400 foreign agencies, as well as media service organizations and sales promotion agencies. Gives, for each agency, name, address (including branch offices), telephone, personnel, major accounts, approximate annual billings and breakdown of billings by media.

G. Directories of Marketing Services

1. American Marketing Association. _Directory of Marketing Services and Membership Roster_. (Chicago: published irregularly.)

Lists market research firms and describes their services; also lists individual and corporate AMA members.

2. _Green Book; International Directory of Marketing Research Houses and Services_. (New York: American Marketing Assn., annual.)

Includes basic information, principal personnel, and a description of services for U.S. and international marketing firms.

3. _Bradford's Directory of Marketing Research Agencies and Management Consultants in the United States and the World_. (Fairfax, VA: biennial.)

Gives name, address and services available for over 500 market research and management consultant firms in the U.S., Canada and abroad.

4. Weiner, Richard. _Professional's Guide to Public Relations Services_. (Englewood Cliffs, NJ: Prentice Hall, 1971.)

Covers agencies managing prize contests, clipping bureaus, mailing services, celebrity agencies, television and radio work, skywriting and other types of publicity. Gives names, addresses and descriptions of services.

H. Information Guides

1. _Executives' Guide to Information Sources_. (Detroit: Gale Research Co.)

This three-volume set guides librarians, businessmen and other information seekers to specialized information on 2,300 subjects. Each entry covers a specific business or business-related subject, and refers the reader quickly and accurately to the best sources of up-to-date information: encyclopedias, dictionaries, handbooks, bibliographies, yearbooks, abstract services, indexes, trade associations, professional societies, periodicals, directories, biographical sources, statistical sources, statistical yearbooks, regular statistical publications, price sources, almanacs, manuals, books of tables and financial ratios.

2. _Statistics Sources_. (Detroit: Gale Research Co.)

This book is a comprehensive, up-to-date compilation of sources of government and nongovernment statistics on industries, products, states and foreign countries, etc., including a plenitude of data compiled by various U.S. Government agencies.

162

Other useful publications of Gale Research Company include

Accounting Information Sources.
Building Construction Information Sources.
Business Trends and Forecasting Informaton Sources.
Commercial Law Information Sources.
Computers and Data Processing Information Sources.
The Developing Nations Information Sources.
Electronic Industries Information Sources.
Government Regulation of Business Including Antitrust.
Food and Beverage Industries: A Bibliography and Guidebook.
International Business and Foreign Trade Information
    Sources.
Investment Information Sources.
Packaging.
Public Finance Information Sources.
Real Estate Information Sources.
Research in Transportation: Legal/Legislative and Economic
    Sources and Procedure.
Standards and Specifications Information Sources.
Systems and Procedures Including Office Management
    Information Sources.
Textile Industry Information Sources.
Transportation Information Sources.

3. Daniells, Lorna M.   Business Information   Sources.
    (Berkeley: University of California Press, 1976.)

    This is an excellent source for a wide variety of marketing
    and business information.

4. Coman, Edwin T., Jr.   Sources of Business Information.
    (New York: Prentice Hall, Inc.)

    Guide to reference materials in the fields of statistics,
    finance, real estate, insurance, accounting, management,
    marketing, advertising, etc. Lists for each field the
    principal bibliographies, periodicals, sources of statis-
    tics, business or professional association, handbook, etc.

5. Encyclopedia of Business Information.   (Detroit: Gale
    Research Co.)

    A two-volume set which lists data and sources of informa-
    tion for management.

6. Johnson, H. Webster and McFarland, Stuart W.   How to Use
    the Business Libary, with Sources of Business Information.
    (Chicago: South-Western Publishing Co.).

    This manual is a guide for training in the use of a
    business library.

7. <u>American Statistics Index; a Comprehensive Guide</u> and <u>Index</u>
    <u>to the Statistical Publications of the U.S. Government.</u>
    (Washington: Congressional Information Service, monthly.)

    Covers statistics in all U.S. Government publications,
    including Congressional hearings. In two parts: an
    abstract volume, arranged by issuing agency, which
    describes the statistics available in each publication; and
    a detailed index.

8. Frank, Nathalie D. <u>Data Sources for Business and Market</u>
    <u>Analysis.</u> (Metuchen, NJ: Scarecrow Press.)

    An annotated guide to sources of business data, with
    emphasis on marketing. Includes research services and data
    bases, as well as publications.

II. <u>Basic Statistical Sources</u>

A. Census Data

The Bureau of the Census gathers and publishes vast quantities
of data about the U.S.; much of this information can be used in
making marketing decisions.

Areas in which the Bureau of the Census publishes series of
reports are

> Agriculture
> Construction Industries
> Government
> Housing
> Manufacturers
> Mineral Industries
> Population
> Retail Trade
> Selected Service Industries
> Transportation
> Wholesale Trade

Since each census is a multivolume set, approaching these
statistics can be a formidable task. To acquaint yourself with
census materials, consult.

1. <u>A Student's Introduction to Accessing the 1970 Census.</u>
    (Washington: U.S. Government Printing Office.)

    A publication of the Bureau of the Census which gives back-
    ground information and exercises to familiarize users with
    Bureau of the Census publications and their organization.

For a comprehensive listing and description of census materials,
use

2. <u>Catalog of Publications.</u> Has both subject and geographic
    indexes. Semiannual and annual supplements describe data
    files and special tabulations, as well as new publications.

Specifically for marketing uses, a useful introduction is

3. Measuring Markets; a Guide to the Use of Federal and State Statistical Data. (Washington: U.S. Government Printing Office, 1974.)

   Shows how government statistics can be used in shaping a marketing program; and gives titles and information for federal and state statistical publications covering publication, income, employment, sales and taxes.

To locate information about population characteristics or area statistics, the basic sources are

4. Census of Population. (Washington: Bureau of Census.) The results of the U.S. Census contains characteristics of population and reports on selected areas.

5. Census Tract Reports. Contains detailed information on population and housing by census tract.

To locate comprehensive population data on a large geographical area consult

6. County and City Data Book (196 statistical items for each county or county equivalent) or Congressional District Data Book (a variety of data organized around congressional districts).

7. Census of Housing. Broken down by volume to include: states and small areas, metropolitan housing, city blocks, inventory change, financing, rural housing and senior citizens.

Other useful sources which cover a broad spectrum of topics are

8. Social Indicators: Selected Statistics on Social Conditions and Trends in the U.S. (Washington: U.S. Government Printing Office.) A publication of O.M.B. which presents statistics on health, safety, education, income, housing, population, leisure and recreation.

9. Statistical Abstract of the United States. (Washington, DC: U.S. Government Printing Office, annual.) This volume is a standard summary of statistics on the social, political and economic organization of the United States; derived from public and private sources.

B. Business Census Data

   1. Census of Manufacturers. (Washington, DC: Government Printing Office.)

      Provides summary statistics on such things as output, size and employment of firms by 450 categories.

2. <u>Census of Retail Trade</u>. Data compiled by geographical areas on retailing by kind of business. Data includes number of establishments, sales, payroll and personnel.

3. <u>Census of Wholesale Trade</u>. Data compiled by geographical areas on wholesalers by kind of business. Data are similar to census of retailing above.

4. <u>Census of Selected Services</u>. Similar to census of retailing but for hotels, motels, beauty parlors, barber shops and other service retailers.

For other business activities, check

<u>Census of Transportation</u>, <u>Census of Construction Industries</u>, or <u>Census of Mineral Industries</u>.

5. <u>Survey of Current Business</u>. (Washington: U.S. Government Printing Office).

The statistical section in each issue is a very comprehensive collection of current business statistics. Areas covered include labor, earnings, finance, prices, major industries and general business indicators.

6. <u>Business Statistics: The Biennial Supplement to the Survey of Current Business</u>.

Provides 30 years worth of historical data for the <u>Survey of Current Business</u>.

To locate business census information on a local area basis, use

7. <u>County Business Patterns</u>. (Washington: U.S. Government Printing Office, annual.)

One report is published for each state, giving employment and payroll statistics by county and by industry.

C. Market Data

1. <u>Rand Commercial Atlas and Marketing Guide</u>. (Chicago: Rand McNally and Company, annual, with monthly supplements on business conditions.)

This volume contains over 500 pages of statistics and maps covering every part of the world, together with indexes of over 100,000 cities and towns. Marketing tables present more than 400 statistical items for each U.S. county. Population figures appear for over 60,000 U.S. localities, the majority of which are available in no other publication.

2. <u>Sales Management and Marketing Magazine Survey of Buying Power</u>. (New York: Bill Communications, Inc., annual.)

This is an annual reference book that is a prime nongovernment authority for population, income and retail sales data for cities, counties, metropolitan areas, states, and the United States. It actually includes four annual issues known collectively as the "Survey of Buying Power":

a. Survey of Buying Power.

Part 1 (July) presents population, effective buying income, and retail sales by type of establishment in all U.S. consumer markets. Part 2 (October) gives projections for U.S. and Canadian metropolitan markets, as well as a survey of newspaper and television markets.

b. Survey of Industrial Purchasing Power. (April)

Gives number of plants, value of shipments and other data for major industries in all states and metropolitan areas.

3. Survey of Selling Costs. (February)

Presents data on sales costs for major industries in 79 U.S. markets, compensation of sales personnel and sales support activities.

Much of the data from the first two special issues is also published in

d. The Survey of Buying Power Data Service. (annual)

Presents market data in three sections: part 1, population and household characteristics, effective buying income and total retail sales for all counties in the U.S.; part 2, retail sales by store groups and merchandise lines; and part 3, television market data, and projections by SMSA for population, effective buying income and retail sales.

3. Editor and Publisher Market Guide. (New York: Editor and Publisher, annual.)

This guide contains standardized surveys of over 1,500 daily newspaper markets, with data on transportation, population, automobile registrations, housing, banks, utilities, principal industries, number of wage earners, average weekly wages and principal paydays.

4. Printers' Ink Marketing/Communications Guide to Marketing. (New York: Decker Communications, Inc., published each fall.)

Covers over 100 leading U.S. metropolitan markets, including important local trends and developments, population characteristics, industry and employment, financial activity, sales volume, major media and outlook for the future.

5. Progressive Grocer's Marketing Guidebook. (New York: Butterick Co.)

   Gives market characteristics, statistical information and a directory of major food distribution centers for all U.S. market areas.

6. Marketing Economics Guide. (New York: Marketing Economics Institute Ltd., annual.)

   Presents market information for 1500 cities, as well as all U.S. counties and metropolitan areas. Features detailed breakdowns of population, households, disposable income, type of economic base, and retail sales by type of store. Includes detailed maps.

A useful general guide is

7. A Guide to Consumer Markets. (New York: The Conference Board, annual.)

   Presents fundamental statistics gathered from various sources on population, employment, income, expenditures for goods and services, production, distribution and prices.

D. Industry Data

   In addition to trade associations and trade publications, check

1. Standard and Poor's Industry Surveys. (New York: Standard and Poor's Corp.) A current analysis of about 70 major industries which summarizes recent data and events.

   (Also check major financial brokerages for industry reviews.)

2. Current Industrial Reports. (Washington: U.S. Government Printing Office.) Government reports on such items as sales and shipments of S.I.C. category.

3. U.S. Industrial Outlook. (Washington: U.S. Government Printing Office, annual.)

   Gives both short- and long-term (ten year) outlooks in most major manufacturing industries, transportation, distribution, marketing, communications, and services.

E. Retailing Data

1. Fairchild's Financial Manual of Retail Stores. (New York: Fairchild Pubs., annual.)

   Gives background and financial information for publicly-owned retail firms, including general merchandise, drug, food and specialty chains.

2. Expenses in Retail Business. (Dayton: National Cash Register Co., published irregularly.)

Gives operating ratios for 35 lines of retail businesss, as well as guidelines for such issues as markups and sales-force compensation.

3. Park, William R., and Sue Chapin-Park. How to Succeed in Your Own business. (New York: Wiley, 1978.)

A practical guide to beginning and operating a small business. Appendix 1, "Characteristics of Selected Small Businesses," gives specific operating and financial data for 80 small businesses, primarily retail establishments. Includes a bibliography.

F. Advertising Data

1. Standard Rate and Data Service. (Skokie, IL.)

This series of publications gives personnel, commission, advertising rates and specifications, deadlines, circulation and other information for all types of media. Publications of the service include:

Business Publication Rates and Data (monthly).
Canadian Advertising Rates and Data (monthy).
Consumer Magazine and Farm Publication Rates and Data
    (monthly).
Direct Mail List Rates and Data (semiannual).
Network Rates and Data (monthly).
Newspaper Circulation Analysis (annual).
Print Media Production Data (quarterly).
Spot Radio Rates and Data (monthly).
Spot Television Rates and Data (monthly).
Transit Advertising Rates and Data (quarterly).
Weekly Newspaper Rates and Data (semiannual).

2. Leading National Advertisers. (LNA, New York: quarterly.)

A three-volume service which analyzes advertising expenditures of major corporations. The three parts are

Company/Brand $. Expenditures in six media by company and brand.

Class/Brand $. Expenditure by product category.

Ad $ Summary. List of brands alphabetically with expenditures.

G. Comprehensive Consumer Survey Data

1. Consumer Expenditure Survey Series. (Washington: U.S. Government Printing Office, 1976.) Includes: Interview Survey, 1972 and 1973, and Diary Survey, July 1973-June 1974.

The surveys, done by the Bureau of Labor Statistics for a recent revision of the Consumer Price Index, present average expenditures of American families for products and services. Data is presented by family income, family size and composition; age, race, and education of family head; housing tenure, region and type of area.

2. Study of Selective Markets and the Media Reaching Them. (New York: W.R. Simmons Media Studies, annual.)

   A thirty-six volume report giving the results of a nation-wide consumer survey of approximately 15,000 adults. The annual survey explores demographic characteristics of consumers, readership/viewing/listening habits for advertising media, and use of 500 products and services.

3. Target Group Index. (New York: Axiom Market Research Bureau, annual.)

   A series of fifty reports giving the result of a national product and media market research survey, doing in-depth interviewing of 20,000 adults per year. Classifies users of over 500 products and services by degree of use and brand loyalty. Covers use of all types of media, including a reader quality study for magazines. Gives both demographic and psychographic data for respondents.

H. International Statistics

1. Statistical Yearbook. (New York: United Nations Publications, annual.) Compiles international statistics on population, agriculture, mining, manufacture, finance, trade, education, etc. The tables cover a number of years and references are given to the original sources.

2. Monthly Bulletin of Statistics. (New York: United Nations Publications, monthly.) This is the current supplement to the United Nations Statistical Yearbook.

I. Forecasting Data and Area Economic Projections

1. Predicasts. (Cleveland: Predicasts, Inc., quarterly, with annual cumulations.)

   Gives long- and short-term forecasts for all U.S. industries, according to SIC number, as well as composite forecasts of basic economic indicators. Data is gathered from both U.S. government sources and a large number of business periodicals. The annual Basebook provides annual statistics since 1960 in the following areas: general economics; agriculture, mining, and construction; manufacturing; transportation, communication and utilities; trade and financial services; services; and government.

2. U.S. Industrial Outlook. (Washington: U.S. Government Printing Office, annual.)

Gives both short- and long-term (ten year) outlooks in most major manufacturing industries, transportation, distribution, marketing, communications, and services.

3. Area Economic Projections, 1990. (Washington: U.S. Government Printing Office, 1975.)

A supplement to the Survey of Current Business giving projections of personal income, employment, and population for all areas of the U.S. in 1980 and 1990.

1972 OBERS Projections: Regional Economic Activity in the U.S. (Washington: U.S. Government Printing Office, 1974.)

Projects GNP, employment, and industrial production by state, by SMSA's, and by other geographical division.

J. Trade Publications Statistical Issues

Many trade publications publish statistical summary issues. If not located in the library contact the publisher directly by consulting Standard Rate and Data Service Business Publications Rates and Data. These include:

1. Advertising Age. (Chicago: Crain Communications, Inc.) Journal issued weekly.

"Marketing Profiles of the 100 Largest National Advertisers," issued the last week in August. This issue presents data on leading product lines, sales, profits, advertising expenditures, and names of marketing personnel.

"Agency Billings," published the last week in February. This issue provides data on advertising agencies ranked by their billings for the year.

2. Appliance. (Elmhurst, IL: Dana Chase Publications, Inc.) Publication issued monthly.

"Forecast Report," issued in February. An issue devoted to sales and other projections by products of the appliance producing industry for the coming year.

"Annual Statistical Review," issued in April. A special issue reviewing the sales of appliances and fabricated metal products over several years.

3. Broadcasting. (Washington, DC: Broadcasting Publications, Inc.) Trade journal issued weekly.

Broadcasting Yearbook, published in March or April. A fact book which compiles television and radio facts and figures.

Cable Sourcebook, issued on October. A fact book providing facts and figures for cable television.

4. Business Week. (New York: McGraw-Hill, Inc.) Business magazine published weekly.

"Liquor Sales," published in February or March. An issue which contains an annual survey of the liquor industry.

"Cigarette Sales," reported in December. The issue presents annual statistics on cigarette trends in the United States.

5. Chain Store Age - Super Markets. (New York: Lebhar-Friedman Publications, Inc.) Trade journal published monthly with an extra issue in July.

   "Outlook," presented in January. An article which provides a general preview of the coming year for chain stores.

   "Annual Product Merchandising Report," printed in March. A report on the trends for product sections of chain store merchandising.

   "Annual Sales Manual," published in July. A full issue providing a performance analysis of thirty-five product categories. Facts and charts are based on actual warehouse withdrawal data for stores that do $1 million or more annually.

   "Annual Meat Study," issued in November. A feature article on the status and trends in meat sales.

6. Computerworld. (Newton, MA: Computerworld, Inc.) Journal published fifty-one times a year.

   "Review and Forecast," presented at the end of December. A section of the last issue of each year devoted to analysis of the industry's previous year and the outlook for the next year.

7. The Discount Merchandiser. (New York: McFadden-Bartell Publishing Company.) Journal issued monthly.

   "The True Look of the Discount Industry," published in May and June. Special annual issues which provide marketing and sales facts and figures on the $30 billion discount store industry.

8. Discount Store News. (New York: Lebhar-Friedman Publications, Inc.) Newspaper published every other week and monthly in December.

   "Statistical Issue," published in September. An issue devoted to presenting statistics on apparel, automotive products, health and beauty aids, hardware, housewares and sporting goods sales in discount stores.

9. Distribution Worldwide. (Radnor, PA: Chilton Company.) Magazine published monthly.

   Distribution Guide, published in July. An annual issue compiling information on U.S. shipper associations, container carriers and lessors, a directory of top truckers, air container guide, a piggy-back guide, information for a world ports directory, and a guide to public warehouses.

10. <u>Drug</u> <u>and</u> <u>Cosmetic</u> <u>Industry</u>. (New York: Drug Markets, Inc.) Journal issued monthly.

    <u>Drug</u> <u>and</u> <u>Cosmetic</u> <u>Catalog</u>, published in July. A separate publication which provides an annual list of the manufacturers of drugs and cosmetics and their respective products.

11. <u>Drug</u> <u>Topics</u>. (Oradell, NJ: Litton Publications Corporation.) Journal published twice a month.

    <u>Red</u> <u>Book</u>, published in November. A separate publication which lists all pharmaceutical products and their wholesale and retail prices.

12. <u>Editor</u> <u>&</u> <u>Publisher</u>. (New York: The Editor & Publisher Company, Inc.) Trade journal issued weekly.

    <u>Market</u> <u>Guide</u>, published annually in January. A guide containing standardized surveys of over 1,500 daily newspaper markets in the United States and Canada, with data on automobiles, banks, gas meters, housing, principal industries, population, and transportation.

13. <u>Forest</u> <u>Industries</u>. (San Francisco: Miller Freeman Publications, Inc.) Trade journal published monthly, with an extra issue in May.

    "Forest Industries Wood-Based Panel," published in March. An article devoted to a review of the production and sales figures for fiberboard, hardboard, particleboard, and plywood.

    "Annual Lumber Review and Buyer's Guide," published in May. A special issue presenting a statistical review of the lumber industry including information on forestry and logging as well as the manufacture of hardboard, lumber, particleboard, plywood and other wood products.

14. <u>Implement</u> <u>&</u> <u>Tractor</u>. (Kansas City, MO: Intertec Publishing Corporation.) Magazine published twenty-four times a year.

    "Red Book Issue," published the end of January. A special issue providing equipment specifications and operating data for farm and industrial equipment.

    "Product File Issue," printed the end of March. An issue which serves as an annual directory and purchasing guide for the industry.

    "Market Statistics Issue," presented in November. A special issue giving statistics on the farm industry, changes in farming, tractor usage, farm income, and equipment production and use.

15. <u>Men's Wear</u>. (New York: Fairchild Publications, Inc.) Magazine published twice monthly.

   "MRA Annual Business Survey," issued in July. A summary of the Menswear Retailers of America annual survey which gives trends in sales, markups, markdowns, turnover ratios and breakdowns of stock classifications, by geographic region and for the total menswear industry.

16. <u>Merchandising Week</u>. (Cincinnati, OH: Billboard Publications, Inc.) Journal published weekly.

   "Annual Statistical and Marketing Report," issued the end of February. A special issue which compiles ten-year sales data in units and dollars and household usage saturation for housewares, major appliances, and home elctronic products.

   "Annual Statistical and Marketing Forecast," printed in May. A special issue providing a survey of manufacturers' estimtes for the year's sales performance of housewares, major applicances and home electronic products.

17. <u>Modern Brewery Age</u>. Stamford, CT: Business Journals, Inc.) Tabloid published weekly; magazine issued every other month.

   "Review," published in February. Magazine section reviews sales and production figures for the brewery industry.

   The <u>Blue Book</u>, issued in May. A separate publication which compiles sales and consumption figure by state for the brewery industry.

18. <u>National Petroleum News</u>. (New York: McGraw-Hill, Inc.) Magazine issued monthly and twice in May.

   "Factbook Issue," published in mid-May. A special issue which compiles statistics on sales, consumption, distribution advertising, and marketing trends of fuel oils, gasoline, and related products by company, state, and nation categories.

19. <u>Product Management</u>. (Oradell, NJ: Litton Publication Corporation.) Formerly <u>Drug Trade News</u>. Journal issued monthly.

   "Advertising Expenditures for Health and Beauty Aids," published in July. An annual survey of the advertising expenditures for the industry.

   "Top Health and Beauty Aids Promotions," published quarterly. Articles reviewing the advertising, displays, packaging and other marketing promotions of top drug and cosmetic companies.

20. <u>Progressive Grocer</u>. (New York: Progressive Grocer, Inc.) Journal published monthly.

"Annual Report," issued in April. A special issue reporting sales by size and type of store, industry trends and issues, and operating performance indicators for the grocery business.

21. <u>Quick Frozen Foods</u>. (New York: Harcourt, Brace, Jovanovich Publications.) Trade journal published monthly.

"Frozen Food Almanac," issued in October. A special issue providing statistics on the frozen food industry by products.

22. <u>VENDing Times</u>. (New York: VENDing Times.) Journal published monthly with one extra issue in February and in June.

"The Buyers Guide," issues in February. A special issue providing information for use by the industry.

"The Census of the Industry," published in June. A special issue reporting statistics on the industry, including number of vending machines by type, best-selling brands and company operating patterns.

SAMPLE TERM PAPER

CALVIN KLEIN
AND THE JEANING OF AMERICA

SUZANNE FINNIGAN
Undergraduate Student
University of California—San Diego
1983

INTRODUCTION

Not so long ago, labels were put only on the inside of garments and other products to identify the manufacturer or retail outlet. But times have changed and an epidemic of "signature goods" has broken out. A signature good carries an external brand mark such as a symbol, logo or name that has the purpose of endowing the product with high perceived quality and affiliation with a famous designer in order to create the basis for status and price differentiation. Many people are willing or even eager to flaunt the Lacoste "alligator," the Ralph Lauren "polo-player," the Gucci logo or the familiar Calvin Klein nameplate on their sleeves, breast pockets, luggage, handbags and, especially, their derrieres.

Names such as Yves Saint Laurent, Pierre Cardin, Emilio Pucci, Bill Blass, Diane Von Furstenberg, and Calvin Klein appear on items from women's dresses, sweaters, jeans, handbags and scarves to men's shirts, belts, shoes, and sportswear. Designers have experienced remarkable business success as a result of the licensing of their name and/or designs that most of them engage in. In less than 12 years, 39-year-old Calvin Klein has developed 11 licensees producing a full range of men's, women's, and children's apparel and accessories. One such licensing deal with Puritan Fashions Corporation enabled Klein to lead the transformation of that once mundane garment, blue jeans, into an item of fashion that is now sold in huge volume by high-voltage advertising.

PURITAN FASHIONS CORPORATION

Before Puritan Fashions formed their exclusive association with Calvin Klein in 1978, it had to deal with the ups-and-downs in sales of the lackluster mid-priced apparel market. Incorporated in New York in June, 1958, as Sportempos, Inc. (their present name was adopted in 1961), the company became a consolidation of various low-budget women's apparel divisions and subsidiaries of Reliance Manufacturing Company.[1] Between the years 1964 and 1974, Puritan acquired and sold several subsidiaries and divisions, and as of December 31, 1981, was whole owner of six subsidiaries and seven divisions.[2]

Over a period of years, the company's 40-odd traditional product lines enabled it to establish a leadership position in the apparel industry. It soon became apparent to Puritan management that this position could provide the company with an important advantage in its planned diversification into designer-related apparel, and in 1978, the innovative Calvin Klein jeans line was introduced.

The instant success of these "prestige" trousers priced at $35 — double the price of non-label styles — shocked the apparel industry. Although Puritan had no previous experience in jeans, the company's production soared to 125,000 pairs a week, making it the leader in designer jeans, with a 20% share of the $1 billion retail market it created.[3]

After careful analysis, the company decided to pursue this avenue of diversification. As a result of the dramatically strong demand for this designer-related product, Puritan's new corporate objective was "to become the premier designer apparel marketing company in the industry,"[4] by implementing a three-year program to put a designer's name on every apparel product Puritan made, including dresses, skirts, shirts, and slacks. The company planned to phase out its budget-apparel line sold through 2,000 stores, including such mass merchants as Sears, Roebuck & Co. and J. C. Penney Co., in order to concentrate entirely on medium-priced designer fashions sold through the 350 exclusive stores that carry

Klein jeans. These included the introduction of additional Calvin Klein jeans line for men and children, Calvin Klein western style skirts, and Klein shirts and dresses, as well as signing designer Diane Von Furstenberg to create a line of women's dresses, suits and sportswear for Puritan.

With the posting of "housecleaning costs" of $3.4 million in 1980, Puritan completed the final phase of this bold, three-year transformation of its business. Exhibit 1 illustrates this achievement. The transition from a manufacturer of low margin dresses to a mass marketer of designer apparel occurred simply because sales of the company's Calvin Klein designer jeans for women greatly exceeded all expectations, and thus exposed a great deal of untapped potential in signature goods. The following is a summary of Puritan's unusual achievements with regard to the Calvin Klein line (Exhibit 2 shows these accomplishments graphically):

- In February 1978, Puritan shipped the first Calvin Klein jeans and recorded $19 million in sales for that single product for their first year. These sales represented 13% of their total corporate sales of $147 million for 1978.[5]

- In 1979, Puritan began to broaden their line of Calvin Klein products and sales rose to $60 million or 37% of their total sales of $160 million[6].

- In 1980, sales under the Calvin Klein label grew to $107 million or 66% of their total sales of $162 million.[7]

- In 1981, sales surged to $248 million, attributable to the Calvin Klein division, which accounted for 90% of total sales, about $225 million.[8]

- In 1982, full-year sales declined slightly to $243 million because of high interest rates, lagging retail orders and lower prices. These price cuts caused a decrease in dollar sales of

Calvin Klein division to about $182 million, 75% of total, but unit sales increased 20%.[9]

Calvin Klein has consistently added new products to the lines produced by Puritan which bear his name. Today they stand as a broad-based sportswear collection of tasteful fashion items for the active man, woman and child encompassing an appealing range of popular designer apparel products.[10] The progress demonstrated by Puritan's two designer operations (particularly the Calvin Klein line) has shown the company's ability to enter into a new apparel area after decades in the popular priced sector.

COMPETITORS & THEIR MARKETING PROGRAMS

Just as Puritan initiated the concept of attaching a designer label to otherwise ordinary clothing and hence "changed the destiny of the company,"[11] it was suddenly faced with a new threat: a score of aggressive new competitors began to saturate the new designer-jeans market.

In early 1979, jeans bearing the designer labels of Gloria Vanderbilt, Anne Klein, Geoffrey Beene, and Bill Blass grabbed a major share of the market created by Puritan. Even new jeans companies not affiliated with a big-name designer challenged the Calvin Klein product. One of the more aggressively promoted jeans labels - Jordache - may sound like that of an haute couture designer, but is actually a modified acronym for Joseph, Ralph, and Avi Nakash, the three Israeli brothers who formed Jordache Enterprises in 1978. Similarly, Sasson Jeans, Inc. conceded that its label has designer appeal partly because its name is often mistaken for that of Vidal Sassoon, the hair stylist. Given the finite number of name designers available for licensing, many new manufacturers merely created their own designs and marketed them under "catchy" ficticious names such as Sergio Valente. Today there are more than 500 companies making jeans of one kind or another.[12]

Just 7 years ago designer-denims didn't even exist. The blue-jeans market was dominated, as it still is, by Levi-Strauss & Co.; Blue Bell, Inc., maker of Wrangler jeans; and V. F. (for Vanity Fair) Corp., which markets the Lee brand. The mid-1960's, when the counter-culture adopted blue denims as uniform dress, was the beginning of the jeans industry. Blue jeans were the staple of the anti-establishment 1960's. Levis and Wranglers symbolized self-expression and protest. Charles Reich, in his book, The Greening of America, wrote that jeans symbolized "a deliberate rejection of the neon colors and artificial, plastic-coated look of affluent society."[13] But then in 1978, designer jeans stirred up the market. Blue denim pants were no longer considered anti-fashion. They became status symbols.

Levi-Strauss & Co. and Blue Bell, Inc. claimed that the famous designers only imitated their sturdy and reasonably priced jeans. Regardless, by September 1979, designer jeans had chalked up $1 billion in sales, close to 10% of the total jeans market, even though they were priced almost three times that of traditional jeans.[14] Status jeans were able to carve out a new marketing niche by introducing fashion and prestige to jeans. The jeans industry was being catapulted into a phenomenally successful business.

Of course, the inevitable result was the existence of too many labels battling for increasingly scarce shelf space and chasing after a limited market. The industry soon became over-saturated, and thus effective image advertising became major determinants of a company's success.

Ad budgets for designer jeans far exceed budgets for traditional jeans. It is not odd for even an established designer-jeans maker to spend 10 to 15 percent of sales on advertising to maintain or increase their position in a field of over 500 different brands. That compares to a 1 to 2 percent formula for traditional jeans. As Exhibit 3 shows, media expenditures have included heavy expenditures in consumer fashion magazines, a smaller amount in trade journals and as designer jeans sales grew, companies turned to the medium of television to transmit the message: You can acquire status, and maybe a mate or two, with tight, autographed dungarees.[15]

With the introduction of designer-label jeans, both Levi's and Wrangler's responded to the increasing competitive market. They introduced fashions to jeans and stepped up advertising. Levi's women's wear division spent $6 million in 1979 in advertising, the largest campaign it had ever undertaken.[16] They continued to increase expenditures through the years, and in 1982, Levi's women's jeans division alone spent nearly $3 billion on advertising, almost 15% of total media expenditues for the company. Many of the ads push Levi's straight leg jeans, one of its most popular products and the jean most similar to status jeans. These ads took on the competition directly. Models claimed that the jeans have "my kind of fit. Not tight. Never uncomfortable. Just soft, smooth and very flattering. Maybe you can relax in skin tight jeans. I can't."[17]

The media mix for Levi's women's jeans in 1982 was about 70% TV, 20% magazines, and the remainder used for newspaper supplements and outdoor advertising. TV commercials have generally appeared on spot TV, during late night, prime-time and day-time.[18] The Simmons Market Research Bureau, in their 1980 study of Media & Markets, found that on the basis of the dollar amount usually spent on jeans, penetration of females was highest during these time slots for women spending between $15 and $24 on their jeans. Magazine ads usually appear in such magazines as Cosmopolitan, Glamour, Mademoiselle, People, Good Housekeeping, True Story, Working

Women, and Seventeen.[19]   These are targeted to more conservative, less designer-loyal types of women.

Wrangler's also introduced a tighter-fitting, dressier jean, called Boy Oh Boy. That product didn't have a separate budget, but the Lady Wrangler division increased its ad budget a great deal - 40% in 1979, and another 30% in 1980. Since then, they have reduced their efforts in this line and in 1982 spent only $1,515,100 or about 15% of total media expenditures on their whole Wrangler family jeans division.[20]

The designer jean craze that hit in 1978 has shown just how immediately sales of a status object respond to image advertising. Jordache Jeans, Inc. is perhaps the best example. In 1978, its name in no way inferred status.

Jordache had to popularize its name against widely respected designer names who had entered the market before it had. Jordache built up its name by spending a large share of its revenue on advertising. Although the company had only $20 million in sales in 1978, it undertook an approximate $2 million television campaign, splattering its name in the fashion-conscious New York metropolitan area with 30 TV commercials a week. Jordache had advertised on Good Morning America, the evening news, 11 o'clock news, 60 Minutes, and in prime-time. The company has also advertised in consumer books such as New York Magazine, the New York Times Sunday Magazine, Playboy, Harper's Bazaar, Vogue, Time and Newsweek. By trying to build up its name by only appearing in prestige media, Jordache spends little or nothing on other media such as radio, trade books and outdoor.[21]

Although Sasson Jeans, Inc., which manufactures a tight French-cut jean, looks down upon designer jeans that are advertised heavily, it has increased its advertising budget from $500,000 in 1978 to $2.5 million in 1982 to include television. Sasson advertises on the evening news,

11 o'clock news and Good Morning America, as well as in trade books such as <u>Women's Wear Daily</u>, <u>Daily News Record</u>, and <u>California News Apparel</u>.[22] They also use <u>Vogue</u>, <u>Mademoiselle</u>, <u>Glamour</u>, <u>Gentlemen's Quarterly</u>, <u>Ambiance</u> and <u>L'Officiel/USA</u> to reach their market.[23]

Gloria Vanderbilt Designer jeans for Murjani USA was the first and only designer name on TV in 1978. They felt it was important to talk to the consumers, not the retailers. Gloria Vanderbilt spent $3.5 million or 100% in 1982 in television advertising for its jeans. The ads were placed in the 18 top markets and are concentrated in fringe-time.

Each of these companies has made a major commitment to advertising, which is the prime ingredient of success in the medium-priced designer apparel market. The general concensus among them is that as long as they promote jeans they will grow. Almost all of the TV ads for designer jeans exploit fantasy in campaigns that seem to stretch the principles of truth in advertising. They are not selling a product, they are selling a name that will probably last forever. Television viewers far and wide know the jingles and slogans of Jordache, Calvin Klein, Gloria Vanderbilt and, of course, oh-la-la-Sasson.

APPAREL INDUSTRY

Jeans have enjoyed the longest up-cycle of any product category in apparel history.[24] But with the onslaught of hundreds of status jeans makers, the jeans crowd has become a tiring market with too many manufacturers competing for a piece of it. This over-saturation has had an adverse effect on the jeans market, the great growth just isn't there any more. The recession has also hurt, not only the jeans industry, but also the apparel industry as a whole.

Consumer buying power, interest rates, styles and retailer's attitudes as demonstrated by their purchasing patterns are the major factors affecting the apparel industry. Apparel industry sales increased about 8% in 1981, after jumping nearly 18% in 1980 and 12% in 1979.[25] During the same period, though, disposable personal income gained 11.2%. Exhibit 4 shows that the consumer price index for apparel is increasing at a slower rate than that of all items combined. Exhibit 5 shows graphically that people are spending a smaller percentage of their incomes on their wardrobes than they used to. As a result of the recent decrease in the general inflation rate, apparel purchases are not relatively less of a bargain for consumers. High interest rates over the last 4 years have outpaced the price increases for clothing at both the wholesale and retail levels putting a tight squeeze on profits. Wherever sales increases are being recorded, they are much smaller than those to which the industry had become accustomed.

Any beneficial effects of the 1982 tax cut have been outweighed by the rising rate of unemployement. This has affected the buying power of a large number of Americans. Even those who are employed are feeling insecure about their jobs and are saving money rather than spending. The savings rate grew to 7.0% of disposable income in third quarter 1982 compared to 6.5% year to year.[26]

The reduced consumer demand for apparel is being felt by some parts of the industry more than others. The continued good health of signature goods is under question, since the status-conscious upper-middle class customer is beginning to feel increasingly pinched by the economy and is cutting back on purchases.

As consumer buying patterns are changing, so are retail buying patterns. Because of uncertain demand and high carrying costs, retailers are keeping an even tighter lid on inventory levels. They are placing smaller orders closer to the time of shipment, which shifts more of the burden of warehousing inventories to manufacturer's shoulders. Retailers are also taking longer to pay their bills, increasing manufacturer's normal receivables collection cycle. Thus, many apparel makers are caught in a severe money squeeze: they pay 2-3% above prime interest rate, borrowing against receivables, in order to finance these inventories.[27] If sales don't materialize, they are forced into promotional activity in order to move the resultant backlogs of merchandise. The end result is that profit margins suffer. Another outcome of the late-ordering cycle is the lack of time to test fashion goods. This has resulted in the present inability to spot potential trends, and the unavailability of reorders of anything that could turn out to be a "hot item."

Many apparel firms, due to demand uncertainty, have been forced to maintain a broader base in their product lines. This provides them with at least some protection if consumers suddenly decide to reject one product category. Many of the designer jeans companies have come up with whole wardrobes of casual jeans-related fashions, and have even put their name on products ranging from boots to brassieres. The diversification in the jeans industry began when manufacturers started making status jeans for men, women, and children in scores of colors and fabrics ranging from the various weights of denim to corduroy, velvet, synthetic suede, and stretch denim containing Lycra Spandex for a more figure-defining fit. The newest and hottest variations in the jeans industry are stone-washed and black denim. Apparel makers have begun to scurry to come up with "that special something" that will sell in a resistant market.

Some companies, such as Puritan Fashions, had the foresight to venture into "sportswear," and are now reaping the benefits of doing so. In addition to garments worn for actual recreation, the term "Sportswear" is used to designate all the separate pieces - blouses, skirts, pants, sweaters and blazers for women, and shirts, trousers, sweaters, jackets, etc., for men - that most manufacturers present in coordinated lines and that most consumers buy as individual items to re-coordinate with what they already own.[28] The sportswear category is the main growth area of the apparel industry. The wide range of merchandise and classifications essentially ensures that at any given moment, something is bound to favor with consumers. In addition to Puritan, the major jeans companies, Levi-Strauss and Blue Bell have sportswear lines, and Jordache, Sasson and Gloria Vanderbilt have caught on to this trend in response to maturation of their jeans lines.

At their peak, designer jeans were estimated to comprise no more than 10% of the jeans industry, but their fashion influence had a large effect on primary demand of brand-name jeans. Designer jeans stimulated the market when things were slowing down. The higher price tags on designer jeans both call attention to the "value" of the lower priced basic jeans and provide an umbrella that lets the conventional jeans makers boost prices and fatten profit margins. Most industry observers agree that the domestic jeans market is now probably mature, and demand is expected to stabilize and remain fairly strong.[29] Currently, designer jeans are experiencing a revival at more moderate price points in the $30 price range rather than the original over $40 range. This is more than likely due to the state of the economy, than anything else.

A PROFILE OF THE DESIGNER JEANS MARKET

The demand psychology of the apparel industry should continue to be based, as it has been in the past, on "want" rather than "need." Apparel purchases based on need may be deferrable, but clothing is more than mere body-covering. It is used to express one's individuality (or conformity), status, power, income, and social role. Clothing styles help people create a desired appearance for work, social, or recreational setting. Clothes provide self-gratification.

Exactly who buys designer jeans? And why? These questions were researched in 1981 by Nancy J. Leber, Senior Editor, Harcourt, Brace, Jovanovich, Inc.; Marvin A Jolson, Professor of Marketing, University of Maryland; and Rolph E. Anderson, Professor of Marketing, Drexel University. In an effort to understand consumer acceptance and rejection of currently available signature goods, they conducted a survey to identify and contrast signature goods buyers and avoiders in terms of demographic, personality, sociographic and price-sensitivity dimensions.

The following is taken from the executive summary from that report:.

> Signature goods prone people were identified primarily by their highly aggressive personalities, that is, by a desire for strong interpersonal relationships and a need to be competitively superior by being noticed and admired. Accordingly, this group is more active than others in social and athletic undertakings. They are frequent consumers of alcohollic beverages and gourmet meals, listeners to FM radio or sound systems, and watchers of TV talk shows and crime dramas. They are more concerned about weight control than other consumers. Females, blacks, and well-educated people tend to be over-represented in this group.
>
> These findings suggest that promotional programs should associate signature goods with power, superiority, success, and the admiration one can gain by competing with others in all walks of life. Publicity campaigns and ads should feature celebrities, athletes, or models who are attractive, confident, and successful-looking. The print media should include magazines or publications that appeal to females, blacks, theater- or concert-goers, camera or photography enthusiasts, tennis or ski fans, gourmet food or restaurant devotees, airline passengers, and country clubbers.
>
> The study strongly suggests that signature goods prone individuals view signature goods as symbols of achievement in a highly competitive world. Thus, marketers should consider the sponsorship of TV talk programs where "beautiful people" can be seen, as well as crime shows that coincide with the perceptions that aggressive-oriented people have of the world and themselves, i.e., a fiercely competitive society and a sophisticated winner.[30]

Thus, the propensity for a consumer to purchase signature goods is an increasing function of that individual's aggressiveness.[31] Aggressive people select name-brand products as indicators of social status and reinforcement of their self-concept.

This is very much the case of status-jeans buyers, for having some designer's initials or signature on their back pocket provides maximum exposure of "who" they are wearing, and therefore what "strata" of the social ladder they are a member.

Use of demographics provides many insights into just who it is that relies so heavily on a designer's name for self-gratification. As the postwar baby boom works its way through the population curve, the biggest projected growth in the next decade will take place in the 25- to 45-year-old bracket. The maturing of these postwar babies, the "jeans generation" of the 1960's is associated with such social phenomena as upscale purchasing attitudes, making them the "designer-jeans generation" of the 1980's. This transition of the population is represented in Exhibit 6.

The Simmons study summarizes the characteristics of consumers of jeans by amount usually spent. Age, profession, geographical location, and current stage of life contribute a great deal to the process of identifying the designer jeans consumer. The target consumer of jeans priced $25 or more in general:

- is a female homemaker (83.7%)
- is 18 to 24 years of age (33.2%)
- has graduated from high school only (42.0%)
- is employed full time (49.8%) in a clerical or sales position (30.9%)
- is married (54.3%)
- is white (88.2%)
- lives in a metropolitan suburb (majority in Northeast) (48.7%)
- earns household income of $25,000 or more (42.5%)
- owns a residence (59.3%) valued at $40,000 or more (40.5%)

In order for designer jeans companies to reach this market, they must like any firm, take into account what this average female consumer does in her spare time. In terms of magazines and newspapers, she tends to read those publications wholly intended for her use, women's magazines. Better Homes & Gardens, Family Circle, Good Housekeeping, McCall's, Parade, Reader's Digest, Sunday, and Time are read in large part by women with families who never really had a chance to establish themselves on the social ladder. They are those who were unable to afford designer fashions in the past, and are now able to buy not only the name but the styling at a reasonable price. This is the woman fighting (or dreaming) her way to the top. Those that are already there read magazines only if their hectic schedules permit. When they do, they read magazines such as <u>Vogue</u>, <u>Cosmopolitan</u>, <u>Glamour</u>, <u>Harper's Bazaar</u>, <u>Mademoiselle</u>, <u>Ms.</u>, <u>Town & Country</u>, and others that are strictly regarded as high-fashion tabloids. Because these women <u>know</u> what is fashionable they really don't need to read such magazines, but only do so to check up on the "latest trends." By utilizing various combinations of these magazines to advertise designer jeans, companies can and have penetrated their market so as to reap the benefits of maximum exposure.[32]

The introduction of television advertising to the designer industry has also prompted in-depth studies of when and how much TV status-jeans buyers watch. Most of these women have professions that keep them away from a television from 9:00 a.m. to 5:00 p.m. on average, and because most arrive home to the added duties of preparing dinner and putting the house-hold in order, the majority of them are only able to watch TV at prime-time and in the latter hours of the night. As reported by the Simmons study, a large portion of them probably fall asleep watching the 11 o'clock news, as 29.9% of them were found to watch TV during this time slot. In terms of the actual TV shows they tend to watch, local evening news heads the list, with similar type shows such as 60 minutes and Good Morning America following close behind. Again, daytime shows such as serials and game shows were viewed infrequently due to the fact that most have job responsibilities during this time. Situation comedies had healthy ratings, but in terms of advertising cost per person reached, the informational "magazine" type shows provided the best penetration. As previously stated, most designer jeans companies have opted for this route. It is now generally believed in the jeans industry, that without the large volume television advertising that many firms have taken part in, designer jeans sales would surely have plummeted.

When a customer buys a pair or two of designer jeans that have a wear-time of a few years, by reasons of sheer practicality, would not need to purchase any more for some time. Then why has this business boomed? Repeat buying seems an unnatural thing to do in the jeans market, yet it occurs a great deal. Why? Because of a simple variation on a familiar marketing strategy. The designer jeans companies have established their own designer-loyal customers. It had been thought that once everybody had a pair, designer jeans would lose their status. But this is not so. Women know and trust designers, believe in them and most importantly follow them. A generation ago, stylish women looked to department stores to guide their selection of wardrobes, and each store had its own follow-ing. Almost all the clothes at Saks Fifth Avenue carried the name of the store rather than of a designer. Today, it's the designer's name that counts - Saks Fifth's high-priced ready-to-wear department has become mainly a bazaar of separate designer's shops. Shopping by brand has become more important that ever. With women working, there is less time for shopping, and more reliance on brand and designer. Once a designer's name is on the derriere of a customer, it is usually there to stay.

CALVIN KLEIN MARKETING PROGRAM

When Calvin Klein's designs very suddenly took Puritan out of the bargain basement and into the designer salons, they were left with very little time to consider such tings as product strategy or promotional mix. Luckily for Puritan, by virtue of its name and origin, Calvin Klein jeans did most of the work for them. By letting these jeans lead the way into the eagerly awaiting market, Puritan, in essence, sat back and watched the product establish its own position and pull its own demand. Subsequently, Puritan proceeded with its marketing program standing on a much firmer base.

Positioning the initial Calvin Klein jeans line was like taking a stab in the dark, as they were the first jeans made stylish and form-fitting, not to mention autographed. The anticipation (or expectation) on the part of Puritan of the strong demand for these items was intuitive foresight of the ever-increasing preoccupation with name brands. Puritan and Calvin Klein realized people wanted a garment slightly dressier and better fitting than the standard Levi's or Wrangler's, yet not as fussy or expensive as the designer clothes that were currently available in the mid-1970's. Thus the idea to "dress-up" jeans and "dress-down" designer-wear was born, and the reworking of jeans into a shaplier, more stylish garment, autographed by a big name designer struck gold with the market. The Calvin Klein jeans line virtually established its own position, between the casual and dressy that both wanted a little of the other.

As time went by, and Puritan broadened the Calvin Klein product line into activewear in response to an ever-widening spectrum of consumer tastes, positioning remained at the head of the line, initiating the demand-pull of its market. The designer industry frequently takes this form. Regardless of whether or not a customer really likes a garment, if it has their favorite designer's name written on it, they will regard it as fashionable and will feel "well-dressed" wearing it.

When Puritan climbed the stairs out of the bargain basement, they climbed into a whole new world of luxury stores. This meant a major change in distribution strategy had to occur. Its company salespersons no longer had to plead to get buyers to look over the company's new lines. With designer identification, Puritan could get their products into the stores much more easily. To retailers, status jeans and designer wear can make the difference between a profitable department and an unprofitable one. Through the years, Puritan has constantly added prestigious retail stores to their channel of distribution. These retailers represent a "who's who" of the country's top department and specialty stores.[33] Puritan has also successfully implemented a program to present its diversified product lines in separate Calvin Klein "shops" in the nation's top department stores. thus deepening their direct market penetration and broadening the in-depth availablity of their products.[34] The company currently has 115 Calvin Klein shops housed by various retailers and has plans to add many more.[35]

Having introduced its designer lines into more exclusive stores, Puritan is able to command much higher profit margins than it had previously enjoyed. Exhibit 7 illustrates the increase in gross margin as a percent of sales over the past 6 years. Puritan pays an average of about 6.5% of these margins for royalties on the sales of Calvin Klein and Diane Von Furstenberg products, which leaves a rather healthy pre-tax margin for Puritan.

The profit margin provided by these goods is, of course, a direct reflection of their price structure. Depending on the item, prices of status jeans can range from $35 to $70. In 1979, the average cost to make a pair of basic denim designer jeans was $7.50 to $9, comprising fabric and trim, labor, the contractor's overhead and profit and inspection of the finished product.[36] That cost is doubled or tripled by the manufacturer, who sells to retailers at an average of about $17.50 a pair. The wholesale price includes such items as the licensing fee to the designer, commission to the sales force, the manufacturer's overhead, bad debts and receivables, advertising and promotion costs, and an 8 per cent trade discount traditionally offered to retailers, as well as the manufacturer's profit.[37] Even after adjusting these numbers for inflation, there is some question as to whether or not the mark-up by makers is fair. It may or may not be, but as long as consumers continue to buy the jeans and sports-wear despite the relatively high prices, the companies will continue to implement their pricing strategies. After all, Puritan came up with a good idea at the right time, and they are being thusly rewarded.

The main key to Puritan's success has been its promotional strategy. Like the other designer jeans companies previously reviewed, Puritan spends a relatively large percentage of sales on promotion, both inside and outside the stores. In February of 1979, Puritan hired Vignelli Designs, Inc., a major graphics company, to design special in-store display units for the expanded Calvin Klein line.[38] The units - which came complete with the Klein insignia, customized racks, and even attached dressing rooms - were sold or leased to department stores in the fall of 1979. The displays further distinguish the company's apparel products from those of its competitors and the adjacent dressing rooms lure impulse buyers who often decide against a garment purchase because a dressing room is not available nearby.

Puritan also makes a major commitment to advertising. Designer Klein says that the jeans and other garments that carry designer labels are "not fashion, they're staples." He believes that the key to marketing such items is to promote them heavily as "part of the entire Calvin Klein world."[39] With this rationale, Puritan's initial advertising and media strategies for the Calvin Klein line included Vogue, New York Times Sunday Magazine and Women's Wear Daily. As sales grew to $35 million by December 1978, the company started advertising in consumer magazines like Playboy, Sports Illustrated, Gentlemen's Quarterly, People and Harper's Bazaar.[40] They first advertised in print because they were best known to the people who read. After 18 months in the designer jeans business, their sales volume grew enough to add television advertising in prime, early and late fringe in top markets. Exhibit 8 shows the dramatic increases in total advertising expenditures of Puritan since the designer lines were introduced. The following was taken from Puritan's Annual Report and summarizes the typical Puritan Fashions advertising strategy:

> Our TV commercials, which featured the stunningly attractive Brooke Shields, stimulated both critical acclaim and some controversy. Without question, this medium of TV commercial proved exceedingly effective in communicating our message to millions of consumers around the country. To maintain the momentum generated by that campaign, we have recently released a follow-up advertising program again featuring Brooke Shields as captured by the renowned photographer, Richard Avedon. As before, television will be our dominant advertising medium, supplemented by magazines, newspapers, outdoor advertising and special events. In addition, 60-second advertising features will be shown in 3400 movie theaters in more than 200 cities throughout the country.[41]

The controversial commercials to which Mr. Rosen is referring involved Brooke Shields contorting herself like a pretzel while mouthing suggestive phrases about Calvin Klein jeans. Some television stations refused to air certain Shields' spots. One such commercial included a close shot of the front of Miss Sheids' jeans as she says, "There's nothing that comes between me and my Calvin's." Exhibit 3 shows the 6 media expenditures of Puritan for 1982.

SUMMARY - KLEIN"S COMMITMENT

A relatively young designer, Calvin Klein has triumphed strictly on his sense of design. Other designers court fame by mingling with socialites and selling to the jet set. But Klein has carefully avoided the gossip column route. He even refused to travel to Europe with his fashions.[42] Klein has a secure knowledge of where he fits and why, and that's reflected in his designs.

Luckily for Puritan Fashions, this is the same attitude possessed by their customers. Puritan has been instrumental in building the strong rapport that exists between Klein and his customers. The Calvin Klein image is the most important thing Puritan has, for if he had not signed the licensing agreement back in 1978, the chances of Puritan even still existing are slim at best.

Conveniently, there seems to be little worry that Klein will "defect" from Puritan. He has already purchased 7% of Puritan's outstanding shares. With Klein's involvement secure, Puritan seems destined to remain a leader in the designer clothing industry for as long as one exists.

Needless to say. Calvin Klein is the best thing that ever happened to Puritan Fashions.

EXHIBIT 1

SALES BY TYPE OF APPAREL (000's)

	1981		1980		1979		1978	
Designer Apparel	$248,000	100%	$132,094	81%	$ 82,362	51%	$ 27,162	18%
Non-Designer Apparel	0	0%	30,057	19%	77,973	49%	120,059	82%
	$248,000	100%	$162,151	100%	$160,355	100%	$147,221	100%

Source: Puritan Fashions Corporation Annual Report (1981)

EXHIBIT 2

YEARLY SALES (millions)

Source: Puritan Fashions Corporation Annual Reports (1978, 1981)
         Laura Heberton, "At Puritan Fashions, Calvin Klein Label Spells
         Turnaround," Wall Street Journal (March 11, 1982), p. 44.

EXHIBIT 3

1982 LEADING JEANS BRANDS ADVERTISING EXPENDITURES

(000's)

	Total	Magazines	Newspaper Supplements	Network TV	Spot TV	Network Radio	Outdoor
Puritan Fashions Corp.:	$6,115.1	$1,513.5	$445.5		$3,746.8		$409.3
Calvin Klein Jeans	609.8	196.6			3.9		409.3
Calvin Klein Sportswear	5,080.1	1,229.5	298.6		3,552.0		
Diane Von Furstenberg	425.2	87.4	146.9		190.9		
Jordache Enterprises, Inc.:	16,039.6	2,221.5	1,002.7		12,424.6		390.8
Murjani Int'l., Ltd.:	3,541.5	20.7		$2,629.4	880.1		11.3
Gloria Vanderbilt Jeans	3,509.5			2,629.4	880.1		
Gloria Vanderbilt Sportswear	9.6						9.6
Sasson Jeans, Inc.:	2,527.5	64.8	40.8		2,421.9		
Sasson Jeans	2,164.2				2,164.2		
Sasson Sportswear	246.4				246.4		
Levi Strauss & Co.:	19,214.3	4,973.8	132.9	5,700.1	7,064.5	$839.4	503.6
Levi Jeans	10,999.1	1,492.6	111.9	3,161.7	4,925.7	839.4	467.8
V. F. Corp.:	7,043.4	801.5	214.7	694.1	5,012.7	318.3	2.1
Lee Jeans	4,123.2	100.9	23.1	396.9	3,281.9	318.3	2.1
Blue Bell, Inc.:	10,678.5	623.4	21.0	8,272.8	1,753.4		7.9
Wrangler Jeans	9,431.8			8,272.8	1,159.0		

Source: Leading National Advertisers, (1982).

EXHIBIT 4

CONSUMER PRICE INDEX

(1967 = 100)

YEAR	ALL ITEMS	APPAREL LESS FOOTWEAR
1982	291.3	177.4
1981	272.4	174.0
1980	246.8	167.8
1979	217.4	158.5
1978	195.4	154.2
1977	181.5	150.6
1976	170.5	144.9
1975	161.2	140.6
1974	147.7	135.7
1973	133.1	126.5
1972	125.3	122.3
1970	116.3	116.3

Source: Kenneth W. Clarfield, "Apparel Industry Current Analysis," Standard & Poor's Industry Surveys, ed. Jean Kozlowski (November 4, 1982), p. 102.

EXHIBIT 5

CLOTHING AND SHOE EXPENDITURES

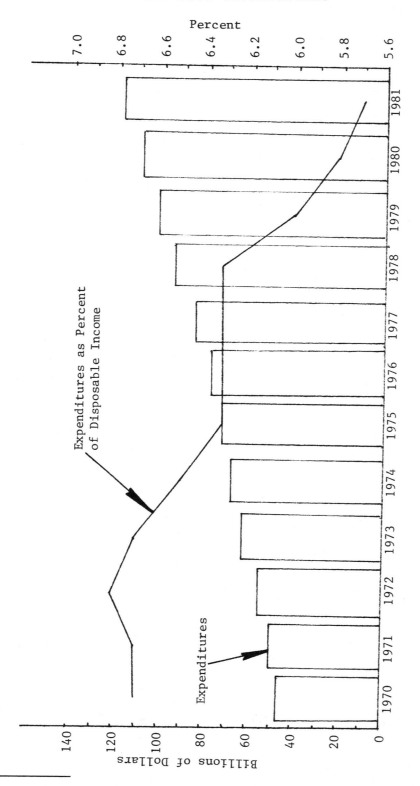

Source: <u>Standard & Poor's Industry Surveys</u>, (1982).

EXHIBIT 6

U. S. POPULATION PROJECTIONS

Age Group (Years)	1982 Number (000's)	1982 % of Total	1986 Number (000's)	1986 % of Total	1990 Number (000's)	1990 % of Total
Under	17,370	7.5	18,462	7.8	19,200	7.7
5 to 14	33,959	14.6	33,380	14.0	35,375	14.2
15 to 19	19,829	8.5	18,405	7.7	16,957	6.8
20 to 24	21,920	8.4	21,282	8.9	18,567	7.4
25 to 29	20,763	9.0	21,878	9.1	21,503	8.6
30 to 34	18,709	8.1	19,961	8.4	22,003	8.8
35 to 39	15,685	6.8	17,821	7.5	20,004	8.0
40 to 54	34,834	15.0	36,580	15.3	43,232	17.3
55 to 64	22,096	9.5	22,207	9.3	21,090	8.5
65 & over	36,833	11.6	28,672	12.0	31,799	12.7
All Ages	231,998	100.0	238,648	100.0	249,730	100.0

Source: Standard & Poor's Industry Surveys (1982).

EXHIBIT 7

GROSS MARGIN AS A PERCENT OF SALES

SALES YEAR	GROSS PROFIT (000's)	GROSS MARGIN ON SALES (000's)	(%)
1978	$147,221	$34,008	23.1
1979	160,335	49,543	30.9
1980*	162,151	49,131	30.3
1981	248,417	91,666	36.9
1982	243,000	97,200	40.0

* 1980 results have been adversely affected by the very low gross margins realized in the final disposition of non-designer apparel group.

Source: Puritan Fashions Corporation Annual Reports (1978, 1979, 1980, 1981, 1982).

EXHIBIT 8

PURITAN FASHIONS CORPORATION'S

ANNUAL TOTAL ADVERTISING EXPENDITURES

YEAR	ADVERTISING EXPENSES	% SALES
1978	$ 1,392	0.9
1979	5,000*	3.1
1980	8,564	5.3
1981	10,854	4.4
1982	14,000**	5.8

* Estimated
** Actual value unknown. Value given represents Puritan's expectations in 1981 of 1982 expenditures.

Source: Puritan Fashions Corporation Annual Reports (1979, 1980, 1981).

SOURCES OF INFORMATION

[1] <u>Moody's Industrial Manual</u>, (1982), p, 5861.

[2] Ibid.

[3] "Puritan Fashions Trying to Protect a Bonanza Built on Designer Jeans," <u>Business Week</u>, (August 13, 1979), p. 68.

[4] Puritan Fashions Corporation Annual Report, (1979), p. 2.

[5] Ibid., (1981), p. 2.

[6] Ibid.

[7] Ibid.

[8] Laura Heberton, "At Puritan Fashions, Calvin Klein Label Spells Turn-around," <u>Wall Street Journal</u>, (March 11, 1982), p. 44.

[9] "Puritan Fashions Corp. Expects to Report Rise in 4th Quarter Net," <u>Wall Street Journal</u>, (January 21, 1983), p. 15.

[10] Puritan Fashions Corporation Annual Report, (1982), p. 2.

[11] "Puritan Fashions: Trying to Protect a Bonanza Built on Designer Jeans," <u>Business Week</u>, (August 13, 1979), p. 68.

[12] Robert Levy, "After Jeans, What?", <u>Duns Business Monthly</u>, (June 1982), p. 76.

[13] Charles A. Reich, <u>The Greening of America</u>, (New York: Random House, 1970).

[14] "Fancy Pants," <u>Marketing & Media Decisions</u>, (September, 1979), p. 68.

[15] Gail Bronson and Jeffrey H. Birnbaum, "Some People Believe That Blue-Jeans Ads Are a Little Too Blue," <u>Wall Street Journal</u>, (October 7, 1980), p. 1.

[16] "Fancy Pants," Marketing & Media Decisions, (September 1979), p. 69.

[17] Ibid.

[18] Ibid.

[19] Ibid.

[20] Ibid.

[21] Ibid., p. 70.

[22] Ibid.

[23] Ibid., p. 71.

[24] Robert Levy, "After Jeans, What?", Duns Business Monthly, (June 1982), p. 76.

[25] U. S. Industrial Outlook, (Washington: U. S. Government Printing Office, 1983), p. 40-4.

[26] Kenneth W. Clarfield, "Apparels Current Analysis," Standard & Poor's Industry Survey's, ed. Jean Kozlowski, (November 4, 1982), p. 102.

[27] Ibid., p. 96.

[28] Ibid., p. 108.

[29] Ibid., p. 106.

[30] Nancy J. Leber and others, "Profiles of Signature Goods Consumers and Avoiders," Journal of Retailing, (Winter 1981), p. 23.

[31] Ibid., p. 31.

[32] The advertising strategies of various designer jeans companies was previously discussed in the section titled "Competitors & Their Marketing Programs."

[33] Puritan Fashions Corporation Annual Report, (1982), p. 3.

[34] Ibid.

[35] "Puritan Fashions Corp. Expects to Report Rise in 4th Quarter Net," Wall Street Journal, (January 21, 1983), p. 15.

[36] Barbara Ettorre, "Status Jeans: Lucrative Craze," The New York Times, (June 25, 1979), p. D2.

[37] Ibid.

[38] "Puritan Fahsions: Trying to Protect a Bonanza Built on Designer Jeans," Business Week, (August 13, 1979), p. 68.

[39] Ibid.

[40] "Fancy Pants," Marketing & Media Decisions, (September 1979), p.71.

[41] Puritan Fashions Corporation Annual Report, (1981), p. 3.

[42] Walter McQuade, "The Businessman Behind Calvin Klein," Fortune, (November 17, 1980), p. 106.

APPENDIX

U.S.A. STATISTICS IN BRIEF, 1982-1983

Population	Unit	1970	1975	1979	1980	1981
Total, incl. Armed Forces abroad	Mil.	204.4	216.0	225.1	227.0	229.8
Resident population	Mil.	203.3	215.5	224.6	226.5	229.3
Per square mile	No.	57.4	60.9	63.4	64.0	64.8
Under 5 years old	Mil.	17.2	16.1	16.1	16.3	16.9
5–17 years old	Mil.	52.5	51.0	48.0	47.4	46.2
18 years old and over	Mil.	133.5	148.3	160.5	162.8	166.1
25–34 years old	Mil.	24.9	31.3	36.0	37.1	38.8
35–44 years old	Mil.	23.1	22.8	25.1	25.6	26.5
45–64 years old	Mil.	41.8	43.8	44.4	44.5	44.5
65 years old and over	Mil.	20.0	22.7	25.1	25.5	26.3
Median age	Yr.	28.0	28.7	29.8	30.0	30.3
Male	Mil.	98.9	104.9	109.1	110.0	111.4
Female	Mil.	104.3	110.6	115.4	116.5	117.9
White	Mil.	178.1	187.2	193.7	194.8	196.6
Black	Mil.	22.6	24.7	26.3	26.6	27.2
Percent of resident population	Pct.	11.1	11.5	11.7	11.8	11.9
American Indian	Mil.	.8	(na)	(na)	1.4	(na)
Persons of Spanish origin	Mil.	9.1	(na)	(na)	14.6	(na)
Northeast	Mil.	49.1	49.4	49.2	49.1	49.3
North Central	Mil.	56.6	57.8	58.7	58.9	58.9
South	Mil.	62.8	69.6	74.3	75.3	76.9
West	Mil.	34.8	38.6	42.3	43.2	44.2
Urban	Mil.	149.3	(na)	(na)	167.1	(na)
Rural	Mil.	53.9	(na)	(na)	59.5	(na)
Metropolitan areas (318 SMSA's)[1]	Mil.	153.7	(na)	(na)	169.4	(na)
Percent of resident population	Pct.	75.6	(na)	(na)	74.8	(na)
Central cities	Mil.	67.9	(na)	(na)	68.0	(na)
Outside central cities	Mil.	85.8	(na)	(na)	101.5	(na)
Nonmetropolitan areas	Mil.	49.6	(na)	(na)	57.1	(na)
Males:[2] Single	Pct.	18.9	20.8	23.3	23.8	23.9
Married	Pct.	75.3	72.8	69.2	68.4	67.8
Divorced	Pct.	2.5	3.7	4.8	5.2	5.7
Females:[2] Single	Pct.	13.7	14.6	16.9	17.1	17.4
Married	Pct.	68.5	66.7	63.5	63.0	62.4
Divorced	Pct.	3.9	5.3	6.6	7.1	7.6
Households	Mil.	63.4	71.1	77.3	80.8	82.4
Average size (persons)	No.	3.14	2.94	2.78	2.76	2.73
One-person households	Pct.	17.0	19.6	22.2	22.7	23.0
Families	Mil.	51.6	55.7	57.8	59.6	60.3
Average size (persons)	No.	3.58	3.42	3.31	3.29	3.27
With own children under 18 yrs. old	Pct.	55.9	54.0	52.5	52.1	51.8
White	Mil.	46.3	49.5	50.9	52.2	52.7
Married couple	Pct.	88.7	86.9	85.7	85.7	85.1
Female householder[3]	Pct.	9.0	10.5	11.6	11.6	11.9
Black	Mil.	4.9	5.5	5.9	6.2	6.3
Married couple	Pct.	68.0	60.9	54.9	55.5	53.7
Female householder[3]	Pct.	28.3	35.3	40.5	40.3	41.7
Immigrants	Thous.	373	386	460	(na)	(na)
Rate per 1,000 population	Rate	1.8	1.8	2.1	(na)	(na)

(na) Not available.
[1] Standard metropolitan statistical areas as defined in June 1981.
[2] Percent of total, 18 years old and over.
[3] With no spouse present.

Vital Statistics	Unit	1970	1975	1979	1980	1981
Births, live	Thous.	3,731	3,144	3,494	3,598	3,646
Percent to unmarried women	Pct.	10.7	14.2	17.1	(na)	(na)
Per 1,000 population	Rate	18.4	14.8	15.9	15.8	15.9
White	Rate	17.4	13.8	14.8	(na)	(na)
Black	Rate	25.3	20.9	22.3	(na)	(na)
Abortions	Thous.	(na)	1,034	1,498	1,554	(na)
Per 1,000 women, 15–44 yrs. old	Rate	(na)	22.2	28.8	29.3	(na)
Deaths	Thous.	1,921	1,893	1,914	1,986	1,987
Per 1,000 population	Rate	9.5	8.9	8.7	8.7	8.7
Infant deaths per 1,000 live births	Rate	20.0	16.1	13.1	12.5	11.7
White	Rate	17.8	14.2	11.4	(na)	(na)
Black	Rate	32.6	26.2	21.8	(na)	(na)
Deaths per 100,000 population	Rate	945	889	870	(na)	(na)
Diseases of heart	Rate	362	336	333	(na)	(na)
Malignancies	Rate	163	172	183	(na)	(na)
Cerebrovascular diseases	Rate	102	91	77	(na)	(na)
Accidents	Rate	56	48	48	(na)	(na)
Marriages	Thous.	2,159	2,153	2,331	2,413	2,438
Per 1,000 population	Rate	10.6	10.1	10.6	10.6	10.6
Per 1,000 unmarried women, 15 & over	Rate	77	67	64	(na)	(na)
Divorces	Thous.	708	1,036	1,181	1,182	1,219
Per 1,000 population	Rate	3.5	4.9	5.4	5.2	5.3
Per 1,000 married women, 15 & over	Rate	15	20	23	(na)	(na)
Health						
Life expectancy at birth, male	Yr.	67.1	68.7	69.9	69.8	(na)
Life expectancy at birth, female	Yr.	74.8	76.5	77.6	77.5	(na)
National health expenditures	$Bil.	74.7	132.7	215.0	249.0	286.6
Per capita	Dol.	358	604	938	1,075	1,225
Public, percent of total	Pct.	37.2	42.3	42.1	42.3	42.8
Hospital care	$Bil.	27.8	52.1	86.1	100.4	118.0
Physicians' services	$Bil.	14.3	24.9	40.2	46.8	54.8
Nursing home care	$Bil.	4.7	10.1	17.6	20.6	24.2
Private consumer expenditures for health	$Bil.	41.6	69.1	112.0	129.1	148.5
Met by private insurance	Pct.	37.5	43.6	44.8	44.2	45.0
Index of medical care prices		120.6	168.6	239.7	265.9	294.5
	1967					
Physicians' fees		121.4	169.4	243.6	269.3	299.0
	= 100					
Hospital room rates		145.4	236.1	370.3	418.9	481.1
Persons covered, private health insur.[1]	Mil.	154	162	171	(na)	(na)
Percent of civilian population	Pct.	75.9	76.4	77.8	(na)	(na)
Physicians, active M.D.'s[2]	Thous.	282	338	399	418	(na)
Rate per 100,000 population	Rate	138	156	176	182	(na)
Nurses, registered, active	Thous.	700	906	1,075	1,119	(na)
Dentists, active[2]	Thous.	96	107	118	121	(na)
Hospitals	No.	7,123	7,156	6,988	6,965	(na)
Beds per 1,000 population	Rate	7.9	6.8	6.1	6.0	(na)
Occupancy rate[3]	Rate	80.3	76.7	76.1	77.7	(na)
Days of hospital care per 1,000 persons[4]	Days	1,173	1,255	1,224	1,231	(na)
Bed disability, days per person: Male	Days	5.2	5.4	5.6	5.9	(na)
Female	Days	6.9	7.6	7.8	8.0	(na)

(na) Not available.
[1] For hospital benefits.
[2] Excludes Federal practitioners.
[3] Ratio of average daily census to every 100 beds.
[4] Non-Federal short-stay hospitals.

Education	Unit	1970	1975	1979	1980	1981
School enrollment	Mil.	60.4	61.0	57.9	57.3	56.9
Elementary (kindergarten & grades 1–8)	Mil.	37.1	33.8	30.9	30.6	30.1
Secondary (grades 9–12)	Mil.	14.7	15.7	15.1	14.6	14.3
Elementary & secondary in private school	Pct.	10.8	10.1	10.1	(na)	10.4
Higher education	Mil.	7.4	9.7	10.0	10.2	10.4
Female	Mil.	3.0	4.4	5.0	5.2	5.2
School expenditures, total	$Bil.	70.4	111.1	152.1	169.6	181.3
Elementary and secondary	$Bil.	45.7	72.2	98.0	108.6	116.3
Public	$Bil.	41.0	65.0	87.1	96.4	103.5
Average salary, public school teachers[1]	$Thous.	8.6	11.7	15.0	16.0	17.6
High school graduates, yearly	Mil.	2.9	3.1	3.1	3.1	(na)
College graduates, yearly	Mil.	.8	.9	.9	.9	(na)
Adult persons completed high school[2]	Pct.	55	63	68	69	70

Employment and Welfare

	Unit	1970	1975	1979	1980	1981
Civilian labor force, 16 years old and over	Mil.	82.7	93.8	105.0	106.9	108.7
Female labor force	Mil.	31.5	37.5	44.2	45.5	46.7
Employed	Mil.	78.7	85.8	98.8	99.3	100.4
Unemployed	Mil.	4.1	7.9	6.1	7.6	8.3
Unemployment rate	Pct.	4.9	8.5	5.8	7.1	7.6
White	Pct.	4.5	7.8	5.1	6.3	6.7
Black and other	Pct.	8.2	13.8	11.3	13.1	14.2
Male	Pct.	4.4	7.9	5.1	6.9	7.4
Female	Pct.	5.9	9.3	6.8	7.4	7.9
Labor force participation rate:						
Married men, spouse present	Pct.	86.9	83.1	81.6	81.2	80.8
Married women, spouse present	Pct.	40.8	44.4	49.3	50.1	51.0
With children under 6 years	Pct.	30.3	36.7	43.3	45.1	47.8
Weekly earnings in private industry	Dol.	120	164	220	235	255
Manufacturing	Dol.	134	191	269	289	318
Services	Dol.	97	135	175	191	209
Retail trade	Dol.	82	109	139	147	158
Index of productivity[3][4]	1977	86.2	94.7	99.6	98.9	100.7
Index of compensation per hour[3]	= 100	58.2	85.5	119.1	131.4	144.1
Labor organization membership	Mil.	21.8	[5]23.4	[6]23.3	22.8	(na)
Percent of nonfarm employed	Pct.	30.8	[5]29.9	[6]26.9	25.2	(na)
Public social welfare expenditures	$Bil.	145.9	290.0	428.3	(na)	(na)
Percent Federal	Pct.	53.0	57.7	61.7	(na)	(na)
Social insurance	$Bil.	54.7	123.0	193.6	(na)	(na)
Medicare	$Bil.	7.1	14.8	29.2	(na)	(na)
Education	$Bil.	50.8	80.9	108.3	(na)	(na)
Social Security beneficiaries	Mil.	26.2	32.1	35.1	35.6	36.0
Total payments	$Bil.	31.9	66.9	104.3	120.5	141.0
Avg. monthly benefit,[7] 1981 dol.	Dol.	276	350	368	376	386
Medicaid: Recipients	Mil.	14.5	22.2	21.3	21.6	22.1
Total payments	$Bil.	4.8	12.3	20.5	23.3	27.3
Food stamps: Participants	Mil.	6.5	19.2	19.3	22.0	22.2
Federal Govt. cost	$Bil.	.6	4.4	6.5	8.7	10.6
A.F.D.C.:[8] Recipients	Mil.	9.7	11.4	10.4	11.1	10.5
Total payments	$Bil.	4.9	9.2	11.1	12.5	(na)

(na) Not available.
[1] Elementary and secondary schools only.
[2] Persons 25 years old and over.
[3] In private economy.
[4] Output per paid hour.
[5] 1974 data.
[6] 1978 data.
[7] Retired worker.
[8] Aid to Families with Dependent Children program.

Income and Prices	Unit	1970	1975	1979	1980	1981
Gross national product (GNP)	$Bil.	993	1,549	2,418	2,633	2,938
Per capita	Dol.	4,841	7,173	10,741	11,566	12,780
Personal consumption expenditures	$Bil.	622	976	1,507	1,667	1,843
Gross private domestic investment	$Bil.	144	206	423	402	472
Net exports of goods and services	$Bil.	7	27	13	25	26
Govt. purchases of goods and services	$Bil.	220	340	474	538	597
National income	$Bil.	811	1,239	1,967	2,117	2,353
Personal income	$Bil.	811	1,265	1,951	2,160	2,416
Disposable personal income	$Bil.	695	1,096	1,650	1,824	2,029
Per capita	Dol.	3,390	5,075	7,331	8,012	8,827
Personal savings	$Bil.	56	94	97	106	130
GNP, constant (1972) dollars	$Bil.	1,086	1,232	1,479	1,474	1,503
Per capita	Dol.	5,293	5,702	6,572	6,475	6,537
GNP implicit price deflator, index	1972 = 100	91.5	125.8	163.4	178.6	195.5
Median family money income	Dol.	9,867	13,719	19,587	21,023	22,388
White families	Dol.	10,236	14,268	20,439	21,904	23,517
Black families	Dol.	6,279	8,779	11,574	12,674	13,266
Median family income, 1981 dollars	Dol.	23,111	23,183	24,540	23,204	22,388
Families below poverty level	Mil.	5.3	5.5	5.5	6.2	6.9
Percent of all families	Pct.	10.1	9.7	9.2	10.3	11.2
Persons below poverty level	Mil.	25.4	25.9	26.1	29.3	31.8
Percent of all persons	Pct.	12.6	12.3	11.7	13.0	14.0
Producer price index (PPI):[1]						
Crude materials		112.3	196.9	274.3	304.6	329.0
Fuel	1967	122.6	271.5	507.6	615.0	751.2
Immediate materials	= 100	109.9	180.0	243.2	280.3	306.0
Finished goods		110.3	163.4	217.7	247.0	269.8
PPI, all commodities		110.4	174.9	235.6	268.8	293.4
Consumer price index, all items		116.3	161.2	217.4	246.8	272.4
Fuel oil, coal and bottled gas		110.1	235.3	403.1	556.0	675.9
Homeownership cost[2]		128.5	181.8	262.4	314.0	352.7
Gas and electricity	1967	107.3	169.6	257.8	301.8	345.9
Medical care	= 100	120.6	168.6	239.7	265.9	294.5
Transportation		112.7	150.6	212.0	249.7	280.0
Food		114.9	175.4	234.5	254.6	274.6
Rent		110.1	137.3	176.0	191.6	208.2
Urban intermediate budget:						
4-person family	$Thous.	10.7	15.3	20.5	23.1	25.4
Retired couple	$Thous.	4.5	6.5	8.6	9.4	10.2

[1] By stage of processing.

[2] Includes home purchase, interest, taxes, insurance, maintenance, and repairs.

Business and Finance	Unit	1970	1975	1979	1980	1981
Proprietorships and partnerships, number	Mil.	10.3	12.0	13.6	(na)	(na)
Receipts	$Bil.	331	486	746	(na)	(na)
Corporations, number active	Mil.	1.7	2.0	2.6	(na)	(na)
Receipts	$Bil.	1,751	3,199	5,599	(na)	(na)
Index of net business formation	1967	107	109	132	121	113
Industrial production index	= 100	108	118	153	147	151
Manufacturing output related to capacity	Pct.	79	73	86	79	79
Value added by manufacture	$Bil.	300	442	748	773	(na)
Average employment in manufacturing	Mil.	19	18	21	21	(na)
Raw steel production, short tons	Mil.	132	117	136	112	121
Manufacturing and trade sales, avg., mo.	$Bil.	107	182	295	322	351
Mfg. and trade inventories (Dec. 31)	$Bil.	178	288	444	483	520
Inventory-sales ratio	Ratio	1.62	1.57	1.43	1.45	1.43
Retail stores, sales	$Bil.	368	588	894	952	1,039
Gross private domestic investment	$Bil.	144	206	423	402	472
In constant (1972) dollars	$Bil.	159	155	236	208	226
Expenditures for new plant and equipment	$Bil.	105.6	157.7	270.5	295.6	321.5
Corporate profits after taxes	$Bil.	41.3	81.5	165.1	157.8	150.9
Corporate capital consumption allowances	$Bil.	56.6	89.4	142.7	163.4	189.4
Profit to stock equity ratio, mfg. corp.	Pct.	9.3	11.6	16.5	13.9	13.6
Mergers, mfg. and mining concerns	Thous.	1.4	.4	.5	(na)	(na)
Industrial and commercial failures	Thous.	10.7	11.4	7.6	11.7	16.8
Current liabilities	$Bil.	1.9	4.4	2.7	4.6	7.0
New construction, value	$Bil.	95	136	230	231	238
Residential, incl. farm	$Bil.	32	46	99	87	87
In constant (1977) dollars	$Bil.	168	152	179	161	156
New housing units started	Thous.	1,469	1,171	1,760	1,313	1,100
Commercial banks: Assets	$Bil.	582	975	1,438	1,544	1,692
Loans, gross	$Bil.	300	513	814	842	933
Deposits	$Bil.	486	793	1,109	1,194	1,278
Savings and loan assns: Assets	$Bil.	176	338	579	631	664
Savings capital	$Bil.	146	286	470	512	524
Demand deposits and currency	$Bil.	215	288	368	383	359
Time deposits[1]	$Bil.	413	729	1,075	1,151	1,199
Credit market debt outstanding	$Bil.	1,946	2,620	4,235	4,652	5,118
Consumer credit outstanding	$Bil.	143	223	377	385	410
Mortgage debt outstanding	$Bil.	474	802	1,327	1,446	1,545
Residential nonfarm	Pct.	75.5	73.7	76.0	75.9	75.2
Money market rates: Corporate bonds Aaa	Pct.	8.04	8.83	9.63	11.94	14.17
Treasury bills, 3-month	Pct.	6.39	5.77	10.07	11.43	14.03
Home mortgages, conventional, new	Pct.	8.52	9.10	11.15	13.95	16.52
Prime rate charged by banks	Pct.	7.9	7.9	12.7	15.3	18.9
NYSE common stock index, mo. avg.[2]	Index	46	46	58	68	74
Dow-Jones industrial (30 stocks), mo. avg., dol. per share	Dol.	753	803	844	891	933
Mutual funds, assets	$Bil.	48	46	95	135	241
Life insurance companies: Assets	$Bil.	207	289	432	479	526
Life insurance in force	$Bil.	1,402	2,140	3,222	3,541	4,064

(na) Not available.
[1] Savings and small denomination time deposits.
[2] Index base: Dec. 31, 1965 = 50.

Agriculture	Unit	1970	1975	1979	1980	1981
Farm population[1]	Mil.	9.7	8.9	7.6	7.2	6.9
Farms[2]	Thous.	[1]2,949	2,521	2,430	2,428	2,434
Average acres per farm[2]	No.	[1]374	420	429	429	428
Gross farm income	$Bil.	58.7	101.0	151.3	150.6	166.8
Crops	$Bil.	21.0	45.8	63.1	71.7	75.0
Livestock	$Bil.	29.5	43.1	68.6	67.8	68.5
Net farm income	$Bil.	14.2	25.2	32.3	20.1	25.1
Average per farm[2]	$Thous.	[1]4.8	10.0	13.3	8.3	10.3
Farm output per unit of total input, index	1967 = 100	102	115	119	115	126
Crop production per acre, index	1977 = 100	88	96	113	99	114
Corn production, bushels	Bil.	4.2	5.8	7.9	6.6	8.2
Wheat production, bushels	Bil.	1.4	2.1	2.1	2.4	2.8
Beef production, pounds	Bil.	21.7	24.0	21.4	21.6	22.4
Communication and Transportation						
Postal service revenues	$Bil.	7.7	11.6	18.0	19.1	20.8
Postal service surplus (+) or deficit (−)	Mil.	− 165	− 988	+ 470	− 306	− 588
Pieces of mail per capita	No.	412	415	452	475	477
Telephone systems, operating revenues	$Bil.	18.2	31.3	49.8	55.6	(na)
Cable television subscribers	Mil.	4.5	9.8	14.1	16.0	18.3
Commercial broadcast revenues:[3] Radio	$Bil.	1.1	1.7	2.9	3.2	(na)
Television	$Bil.	2.8	4.1	7.9	8.8	(na)
Daily newspapers	No.	1,748	1,756	1,763	1,745	1,730
Net paid circulation	Mil.	62.1	60.7	62.2	62.2	61.4
Highway mileage, total	Thous.	3,730	3,838	3,918	3,955	(na)
Motor vehicle registrations	Mil.	108	133	152	156	160
New pass. car sales:[4] Domestic	Mil.	7.1	7.1	8.3	6.6	6.2
Imports	Mil.	1.3	1.6	2.3	2.4	2.3
Intercity passenger traffic[5]	Bil.	1,185	1,359	1,589	1,559	(na)
By private automobiles	Pct.	86.6	86.2	83.2	83.4	(na)
Intercity freight traffic[6]	Bil.	1,936	2,066	2,572	2,503	(na)
Moved by railroads	Pct.	39.8	36.7	36.0	37.2	(na)
Cargo tonnage of waterborne commerce	Mil.	1,532	1,695	2,074	1,999	(na)
Operating revenues: Railroads[7]	$Bil.	12.0	16.4	25.2	28.1	30.9
Domestic air carriers[8]	$Bil.	7.1	11.9	21.3	26.4	29.0
Revenue passengers: Domestic airlines[8]	Mil.	153	189	293	273	265
Bus lines, intercity	Mil.	401	351	368	365	375
Local transit	Mil.	5,932	5,643	6,370	6,358	(na)
Foreign Commerce						
Balance on current account	$Bil.	2.3	18.3	− .5	1.5	4.5
Balance on merchandise trade	$Bil.	2.6	9.0	− 27.3	− 25.3	− 27.9
U.S. direct investment abroad	$Bil.	75.5	124.1	187.9	215.6	227.3
Foreign direct investment in U.S.	$Bil.	13.3	27.7	54.5	68.4	89.8
U.S. foreign economic and military aid	$Bil.	6.6	6.9	13.8	9.7	10.6
Domestic exports of merchandise	$Bil.	42.6	106.6	178.6	216.6	229.0
Agricultural	$Bil.	7.3	21.9	34.7	41.2	43.3
Machinery	$Bil.	11.7	29.2	45.9	57.3	64.4
General imports of merchandise	$Bil.	40.0	96.6	206.3	244.9	261.3
Petroleum and products	$Bil.	2.8	24.8	56.0	77.6	75.6

(na) Not available.
[1] Based on 1969 census farm definition.
[2] Beginning 1975, based on 1974 census farm definition.
[3] Net revenues.
[4] Retail sales. Imports exclude domestic models produced in Canada.
[5] Passenger-miles.
[6] Ton-miles.
[7] Class 1 only.
[8] Certificated route carriers only.

Selected Data—Regions and States

Region, State	Rank	Population,[1] 1981 Total (mil.)	Per sq. mi.[2]	Population,[3] 1980 Total (mil.)	Percent Black	Percent Spanish origin	Metropolitan areas[4] (percent)	Percent households owner occupied,[3] 1980	Total crime rate,[5] 1981	Unemployment rate, 1981 (percent)	Personal income per capita, 1981 (dol.)
U.S.	(x)	229.3	65	226.5	11.7	6.4	74.8	64.4	5,800	7.6	10,517
Northeast	(x)	49.3	303	49.1	9.9	5.3	85.0	59.0	5,678	7.4	11,212
No. Central	(x)	58.9	78	58.9	9.1	2.2	70.9	68.8	5,247	8.6	10,570
South	(x)	76.9	88	75.4	18.6	5.9	66.8	67.0	5,497	7.1	9,586
West	(x)	44.2	25	43.2	5.2	14.5	82.5	60.3	7,203	7.4	11,291
Ala.	22	3.9	77	3.9	25.6	.9	62.0	70.1	4,899	10.7	8,200
Alaska	50	.4	1	.4	3.4	2.4	43.4	58.3	6,595	9.3	14,190
Ariz.	29	2.8	25	2.7	2.8	16.2	75.1	68.3	7,614	6.1	9,693
Ark.	33	2.3	44	2.3	16.3	.8	39.2	70.5	3,796	9.1	8,042
Calif.	1	24.2	155	23.7	7.7	19.2	94.9	55.9	7,690	7.4	12,057
Colo.	27	3.0	29	2.9	3.5	11.8	80.9	64.5	7,353	5.5	11,142
Conn.	25	3.1	643	3.1	7.0	4.0	88.3	63.9	5,837	6.2	12,995
Del.	47	6	310	.6	16.1	1.6	67.0	69.1	6,689	7.9	11,279
D.C.	(x)	.6	(6)	.6	70.3	2.8	100.0	35.5	(na)	9.0	13,487
Fla.	7	10.2	188	9.7	13.8	8.8	87.9	68.3	8,032	6.8	10,050
Ga.	12	5.6	96	5.5	26.8	1.1	60.0	65.0	5,629	6.4	8,960
Hawaii	39	1.0	153	1.0	1.8	7.4	79.0	51.7	6,543	5.4	11,096
Idaho	40	1.0	12	.9	.3	3.9	18.3	72.0	4,531	7.6	8,906
Ill.	5	11.5	206	11.4	14.7	5.6	81.0	62.6	4,950	8.5	11,479
Ind.	13	5.5	152	5.5	7.6	1.6	69.8	71.7	4,540	10.1	9,656
Iowa	28	2.9	52	2.9	1.4	.9	40.1	71.8	4,717	6.9	10,149
Kans.	32	2.4	29	2.4	5.3	2.7	46.8	70.2	5,404	4.2	10,870
Ky.	23	3.7	92	3.7	7.1	.7	44.5	70.0	3,532	8.4	8,455
La.	18	4.3	97	4.2	29.4	2.4	63.4	65.5	5,268	8.4	9,486
Maine	38	1.1	37	1.1	.3	.4	33.0	70.9	4,243	7.2	8,655
Md.	19	4.3	433	4.2	22.7	1.5	88.8	62.0	6,558	7.3	11,534
Mass.	11	5.8	738	5.7	3.9	2.5	85.3	57.5	5,835	6.4	11,158
Mich.	8	9.2	162	9.3	12.9	1.8	82.8	72.7	6,854	12.3	11,009
Minn.	21	4.1	51	4.1	1.3	.8	64.6	71.7	4,737	5.5	10,747
Miss.	31	2.5	54	2.5	35.2	1.0	27.1	71.0	3,537	8.3	7,256
Mo.	15	4.9	72	4.9	10.5	1.1	65.3	69.6	5,351	7.7	9,876
Mont.	44	.8	5	.8	.2	1.3	24.0	68.6	5,019	6.9	9,676
Nebr.	35	1.6	21	1.6	3.1	1.8	44.1	68.4	4,178	4.1	10,296
Nev.	43	.8	8	.8	6.4	6.7	82.0	59.6	8,592	7.1	11,633
N.H.	42	.9	104	.9	.4	.6	50.7	67.6	4,322	5.0	10,073
N.J.	9	7.4	991	7.4	12.6	6.7	91.4	62.0	6,180	7.3	12,115
N. Mex.	37	1.3	11	1.3	1.8	36.6	42.3	68.1	6,201	7.3	8,654
N.Y.	2	17.6	372	17.6	13.7	9.5	90.1	48.6	6,905	7.6	11,440
N.C.	10	6.0	122	5.9	22.4	1.0	52.7	68.4	4,520	6.4	8,679
N. Dak.	46	.7	9	.7	.4	.6	35.9	68.7	2,991	5.0	10,525
Ohio	6	10.8	263	10.8	10.0	1.1	80.3	68.4	5,447	9.6	10,371
Okla.	26	3.1	45	3.0	6.8	1.9	58.5	70.7	4,837	3.6	10,210
Oreg.	30	2.7	28	2.6	1.4	2.5	64.9	65.1	7,037	9.9	9,991
Pa.	4	11.9	264	11.9	8.8	1.3	81.9	69.9	3,683	8.4	10,373
R.I.	41	1.0	903	.9	2.9	2.1	92.2	58.8	5,852	7.6	10,466
S.C.	24	3.2	105	3.1	30.4	1.1	59.8	70.2	5,319	8.4	8,050
S. Dak.	45	.7	9	.7	.3	.6	15.8	69.3	3,013	5.1	8,793
Tenn.	17	4.6	112	4.6	15.8	.7	62.8	68.6	4,311	9.1	8,604
Tex.	3	14.8	56	14.2	12.0	21.0	80.0	64.3	6,050	5.3	10,743
Utah	36	1.5	18	1.5	.6	4.1	79.0	70.7	5,750	6.7	8,307
Vt.	48	.5	56	.5	.2	.6	22.3	68.7	5,061	5.7	8,654
Va.	14	5.4	137	5.3	18.9	1.5	69.6	65.6	4,671	6.1	10,445
Wash.	20	4.2	63	4.1	2.6	2.9	80.4	65.6	6,742	9.5	11,266
W. Va.	34	2.0	81	2.0	3.3	.7	37.1	73.6	2,619	10.7	8,334
Wis.	16	4.7	87	4.7	3.9	1.3	66.8	68.2	4,767	7.8	10,056
Wyo.	49	.5	5	.5	.7	5.2	15.3	69.2	5,132	4.1	11,780

(na) Not available.

[1] Preliminary estimates as of July 1.
[2] Of land area.
[3] As of April 1.
[4] Refers to 318 Standard Metropolitan Statistical Areas as defined June 30, 1981.
[5] Offenses per 100,000 population.
[6] 10,016.